Dimensions of Authoritarianism

Dimensions of Authoritarianism: A Review of Research and Theory

John P. Kirscht
and
Ronald C. Dillehay

UNIVERSITY OF KENTUCKY PRESS

301. 155
K61d

Copyright © 1967
by the University of Kentucky Press, Lexington
Manufactured in the United States of America
Library of Congress Catalog Card No. 67-17850

Foreword

In 1950 a behemoth of a volume attracted wide attention
in psychology and the social sciences. An outgrowth of a
psychoanalytically inspired investigation of anti-Semitic prejudice and protofascist attitudes, *The Authoritarian Personality* captured the imagination of scholars in many fields for
its portrayal of a coherent psychological posture or syndrome
of personality that made psychological sense of diverse
forms of social irrationality. Ethnic prejudice was the initial
target, but the picture of the authoritarian that emerged at
Berkeley from the work of Adorno, Frenkel-Brunswik, Levinson, and Sanford seemed to throw light on much else: on
modes of leadership and followership, on styles and consequences of teaching and learning, on true believers of
various stripes, and, particularly, on what Hofstader has
since called the paranoid trend in political life. Here was a
major attempt to trace in psychological terms the linkage
between personality and ideology. Here indeed was the
most thorough-going attempt yet seen to carry out the

program that Lasswell has proclaimed in *Psychopathology and Politics:* the depth-psychological search for roots of social action in personal motives displaced on public objects, suitably rationalized.

Not merely did the authors of *The Authoritarian Personality* develop and apply this fertile conception (which in the nature of the case could hardly be entirely original with them: Fromm and Maslow, among others, had anticipated their ideas in important respects); they also provided a wealth of evidence, and—most influential, as it later turned out—they presented a measuring instrument, the F scale, according to which willing and accessible people could be scored on authoritarianism. And the chase was on.

For readers and users of the book, it was tough going from the beginning. More a collection of monographs than a systematically organized book, *The Authoritarian Personality* left the reader to dig and sift for himself if he were to arrive at a view of just what the authors meant by authoritarianism. After considerable digging, he might come up with a picture somewhat like this: Authoritarianism characterizes the basically weak and dependent person who has sacrificed his capacity for genuine experience of self and others so as to maintain a precarious sense of order and safety that is psychologically necessary for him. In the type case, the authoritarian confronts with a facade of spurious strength a world in which rigidly stereotyped categories are substituted for the affectionate and individualized experience of which he is incapable. Such a person is estranged from inner values and lacks self-awareness. His judgments are governed by a punitive conventional moralism, reflecting external standards towards which he remains insecure since he has failed to make them really his own. His relations with others depend on considerations of power, success, and adjustment, in which people figure as means rather than as ends, and achievement is valued competitively rather than for its own sake. In his world, the good, the powerful, and the ingroup merge to stand in fundamental opposition to the immoral, the weak, the outgroup. For all that he seeks to align himself with the former, his underlying feelings of weakness and self-contempt commit him to a constant and embittered struggle to prove to himself and others that he really belongs to the strong and good, and that his ego-alien impulses, which he represses, belong to the weak and bad.

As soon as the book appeared, controversy began. Some, such as Solomon Asch, objected to the one-sided irrationalism of the view of social man that was portrayed. Others, like Shils and, later, Rokeach, quarrelled with the left-liberalism of the authors that had led them to aim their sights at the rightist rather than leftist variants of authoritarianism. And many followed the lead of Hyman and Sheatsley in pointing to technical inadequacies of research method that, taken seriously, rather thoroughly undermined the evidential base on which the book was written. Already in 1954, an entire volume edited by Christie and Jahoda was devoted to a full-dress review of *The Authoritarian Personality*. The psychological literature of the 1950's continued to be full of studies using the F scale and related measures, many of them addressed to methodological problems bequeathed to the field by shortcomings in the original research.

Yet in spite of the critical guns trained on *The Authoritarian Personality*, which time and again found their mark, behemoth refused to keel over. Weak in evidence as it turned out to be, the book remained rich in conception and fertile in implication. Intolerably long, sprawling, and virtually unreadable as a totality, it proved bigger than the swarm of critical studies that one would have thought would destroy it. And evidence kept coming in that lent support to aspects of its underlying conceptions. It has rightly joined the elect of classics in paperback.

How, though, are we to read it, after nearly two decades of research and criticism? The history that I have sketched so lightly presents the student and social scientist of today with a difficult situation. If the original book was hard to digest, the massive literature that followed upon it is by now quite indigestible. As nature takes its course in this state of affairs, the result is not good. Political scientists, educators, historians, sociologists, and others outside the psychological fraternity are likely to throw up their hands, and accept or reject the original formulations as suits their fancy, unguided by the accumulating evidence. Psychologists, on their part, have become bored with the rather arid literature of methodologically-oriented studies of the F scale, and fashion has turned elsewhere, before many of the important substantive problems raised by *The Authoritarian Personality* have been properly resolved. There is the risk that in becoming a classic, *The Authoritarian Personality* may have been stranded out of contact with the steady flow of test and reformulation that constitutes scientific advance.

At this juncture, Kirscht and Dillehay have performed a most useful service that puts the rest of us deeply in their debt. They have set out to digest the indigestible; to provide us with a selective guide to the accumulated literature on authoritarianism and a judicious appraisal of what it has added up to. Their careful review should go far toward correcting the state of affairs that I have just been deploring. To psychologists and other social scientists alike, it should make the accumulation of scattered research findings cumulatively available. And as the period of primarily methodological studies—stimulated by inadequacies

FOREWORD

in the parent volume—draws to a close, it should provide a favorable basis for a new trend in research: to carry forward the unfinished task of reformulating and transforming the insights of *The Authoritarian Personality* into well-grounded understanding.

Berkeley, California   M. BREWSTER SMITH
August, 1966

Preface

For sheer quantity of research and wealth of findings, few areas within the behavioral sciences can rival the study of authoritarianism. Since the delineation of the concept in *The Authoritarian Personality* by Adorno and his colleagues, and, perhaps more importantly, the presentation of a scale to measure authoritarianism, scholars and researchers in a variety of disciplines have directed their attention to this area of research and theory. As recent issues of social psychological and related journals attest, the volume of production on this topic continues.

Existing reviews of authoritarianism describe much of the literature prior to 1956, covering studies that appeared in the five or six years immediately following the work at Berkeley. Since that time a great many studies have appeared, spread over a wide range of subject areas. The person interested in authoritarianism, whether as an area of potential research or for reasons of social concern, faces the task of charting a trip through a vast and scattered domain. In this book we attempt to organize and evaluate the many works dealing with authoritarianism and present them in a coherent, ordered fashion. Given the coverage of previous reviews, our concentration has been on work since 1956.

Categorization of studies by manifest content areas forms the basic organizational scheme for the review. Where relevant we make distinctions among studies treating authoritarianism as an antecedent variable, as a consequence, or as a correlated factor. Throughout we have focused some attention on methodology because of its bearing on the interpretation of results. We have not attempted a major reformulation of the concept of authoritarianism. Rather, we have tried to present an informative evaluation of the current state of knowledge in the area in the hope that by assessing current strengths and weaknesses in the literature we raise issues of significance to current understanding and future work.

We have limited our review, primarily, to social psychological literature: authoritarianism as related to social stratification, beliefs and attitudes, certain personality variables, group processes, leadership, and organizational functioning. We have omitted, for the most part, clinical studies and "purely" personality studies. Most of the studies included in this review used the F scale or a variant of it.

Because of the extraordinary diversity of research and writing on the subject of authoritarianism, coverage of the literature has a certain haphazard quality. Insofar as the coverage was systematic, the main reference works were *Psychological Abstracts*, the *Annual Review of Psychology*, and *Sociological Abstracts*. Much of the material came from the following journals: *Journal of Abnormal and Social Psychology, Journal of Personality and Social Psychology, Sociometry, Human Relations, American Sociological Review, American Journal of Sociology, Public Opinion Quarterly,*

PREFACE

Journal of Social Psychology, Journal of Personality, American Psychologist, and *Psychological Reports.* The bulk of the work discussed here was done in the United States. Some literature of other countries is included, principally that which was abstracted in American journals or available directly. This literature was not extensive but is important. The few cross-cultural comparisons are discussed in a separate section; most of the studies done in other countries are included under the appropriate subject matter headings. Our thanks to Jean-Marie Lemaine and M. C. Vallet of the Laboratory of Social Psychology at the University of Paris for providing us with some European references.

We wish to acknowledge the help and encouragement of several people in the long course of preparing this volume. We began this work at the University of California, Berkeley. Initially, Dr. Dorothy Nyswander provided the impetus for an examination of the authoritarianism literature, but for quite another purpose. We were also encouraged to pursue the matter by Professor Andie Knutson, Director of the Behavioral Sciences Unit at the School of Public Health, University of California, Berkeley, with whom we were associated at the time. It is a pleasure to acknowledge the help provided by Professor Theodore Newcomb, whose comments on the manuscript in earlier form spurred continued labor, and by Professor M. Brewster Smith, both for his encouragement and his critical review of an earlier draft that strengthened the manuscript. Professors Robert Straus of the University of Kentucky and Irwin Rosenstock of the University of Michigan were of assistance in the later stages of the work. We gratefully acknowledge the editorial assistance of Mrs. Elizabeth Holcomb.

December, 1966   J.P.K.
                                                     R.C.D.

Contents

CONTENTS

Introduction

The study of authoritarianism confronts issues of extraordinary social significance, no less today than in 1950, when *The Authoritarian Personality* was published. Dogma, morals, politics, power, childrearing, race relations, organizational functioning—these and more have been explored within the framework of authoritarianism. Social issues that prompted interest in the construct in the 1940's and earlier have recurred in many forms and places; the threat of extremist, authoritarian social movements, whether identified as fascist or not, continues. As a consequence the search for some understanding of the social and psychological antecedents, manifestations, and consequences of this kind of psychological functioning likely will persist.

The promise contained in the formulation of authoritarianism lies in the functional relationship between a variety of beliefs about the world and underlying personality dispositions, joining adherence to pessimistic, hostile, suspicious, antidemocratic beliefs with forces, conflicts, and adjustments in personality functioning. An intraindividual construct,

1

authoritarianism is also decidedly social in consequence and etiology. It is marked by developmental processes, only some of which are even now defined. Certain mechanisms presumably maintain the system more or less intact against forces both within and without. Beliefs and systems of beliefs, theorists believe, reflect at the periphery the central dynamics of authoritarian functioning. Such beliefs exist in social groups and systems, influencing and interacting with social forces. The concern about authoritarianism, perhaps more than anything else, stems from its likely influence on functioning of people in their social activities; authoritarian deeds have more social consequence than authoritarian thoughts.

The history of authoritarianism as a concept in psychology is marked by a rich diversity of interested parties and reveals many different types of investigation. Perhaps this is due partly to ambiguity in defining authoritarianism and the manifold meanings which can be projected into it. But it is due also to the many issues raised by any given piece of research: data inevitably raise as many questions as they answer, questions that extend the initial concept or suggest new leads to understanding it. Some of these questions have concerned the methodological and conceptual implications of response styles in the empirical pursuit of knowledge about authoritarians and nonauthoritarians. The history of the concept reveals stages of initial discovery and outbreak of enthusiasm, criticism and second thoughts, methodological embarrassment and revision, and greater sophistication. Conceptually, the authoritarian personality now has a firm position in psychological theory.

In our organization of material based on the manifest content of research, we start with a review of authoritarianism as conceived by Adorno and his associates. This introductory discussion deals with the nature of authoritarianism

—a problem not yet settled. In addition to a review of commentaries on and criticisms of *The Authoritarian Personality,* a variety of other formulations (such as dogmatism) also are outlined. These represent different emphases in defining authoritarianism with key concepts ranging from emotional malfunctions to social roles.

The theoretical nature of authoritarianism is linked closely to the means of measuring the concept. Since research interpretations hinge on the adequacy and characteristics of the measuring instruments used, we have devoted sections to problems associated with common measures of authoritarianism, particularly the problem of response bias. We include this discussion prior to the presentation of substantive findings because methodological considerations so often influence the evaluation of results.

Next we present studies concerning the identification of authoritarians in terms of social characteristics and cultural subgroups. This section focuses on what may be regarded as the social causes and correlates of authoritarianism, mediated through socialization processes. We then consider some of the important personality characteristics associated with the syndrome, especially cognitive style and emotional concomitants. This portion of the review completes an outline of what authoritarianism is, who are authoritarian, and how authoritarianism developed.

A major portion of the book then deals with the ideological ramifications thought to result from authoritarianism. Certain areas of belief—political, religious, ethnic—have received a great deal of attention in relation to authoritarianism; these represent focal ideological contents that are particularly relevant as social issues. In spite of the number of studies done on authoritarianism in connection with related beliefs, the general conception is relatively straightforward: authoritarianism is treated as a fixed characteristic which affects the susceptibility to certain beliefs. The study of authoritarianism has been a rich source of hypotheses concerning beliefs.

A second major section deals with investigations of social behavior, including both social situations regarded as influential in developing or maintaining authoritarianism and responses of authoritarians to social stimuli. More complex questions involving interaction in small groups, leadership, and functioning in organizations form the final substantive sections. The research reviewed here deals principally with the social consequences of authoritarianism.

As implied in this brief outline, we have found it useful to consider the causal status of authoritarianism in describing various studies. Often implicitly, authoritarianism is treated as antecedent to other variables in many investigations. In others, it is a consequence of prior events. In yet others, it has the status of a correlate. Because it helps clarify and order research findings, this analytical scheme is used throughout when it is appropriate. It also provided a framework for our final summary and evaluation.

I. THE BERKELEY STUDIES

In 1950 *The Authoritarian Personality* appeared, reporting on a series of related studies using questionnaire, interview, and projective techniques. As a result of emerging findings of the exploratory research, what was initially and specifically a study of antisemitism eventually focused upon ethnocentrism and potential fascism. Because of the *ad hoc* nature of the guiding theoretical framework and research applications, *The Authoritarian Personality* was not based on a systematic research program designed to test hypotheses generated by a body of extant theory (Sanford, 1956). To be sure, the work does not withstand critical appraisal by standards of advanced personality research methods and

4

INTRODUCTION

theory (Christie and Jahoda, 1954). The volume did, however, widely influence thinking and research in the social sciences. Its central thesis is that prejudiced and hostile attitudes are expressions of inner needs or impulses which form the foundation of the authoritarian personality syndrome. Certain solutions to intra-psychic conflict result in suspicion, distrust, and hatred of others. This formulation may be regarded as a functional view of prejudiced attitudes.

Within a loosely organized research program, the authors identified potential fascism as an underlying personality complex related to ethnocentrism and antisemitism. The title of *The Authoritarian Personality* is based (Sanford, 1956) on the use of a scale measuring potential fascism (F), developed as an indirect measure of ethnic prejudice to avoid the problems in direct questionnaires. Not merely a product of expediency, the instrument reflects the theoretical scheme evolved by the research team: if prejudice was the result of deep-seated personality needs, then one should be able to assess it without reference to specific ethnic groups. The F scale was developed, then, to measure general prejudice in the personality, not the authoritarian personality (Sanford, 1956).

Stagner (1936) and Maslow (1943) earlier introduced the concept of an authoritarian character or personality structure. According to Sanford (1956), the title was used by Adorno and his associates to draw out the implications of the earlier writing in their own research.

The Berkeley investigators viewed the concept of authoritarianism as a composite of subparts with dynamic relationships to prejudice. As summarized by Sanford (1956, p. 1), these were:

1. *Conventionalism.* Rigid adherence to conventional middle-class values.

2. *Authoritarian Submission.* Submissive, uncritical attitude toward idealized moral authorities of the in-group.
3. *Authoritarian Aggression.* Tendency to be on the lookout for, and to condemn, reject, and punish people who violate conventional values.
4. *Anti-intraception.* Opposition to the subjective, the imaginative, the tenderminded.
5. *Superstition and Stereotypy.* Belief in mystical determinants of the individual's fate; the disposition to think in rigid categories.
6. *Power and Toughness.* Preoccupation with the dominance-submission, strong-weak, leader-follower dimension; identification with power figures; exaggerated assertions of strength and toughness.
7. *Destructiveness and Cynicism.* Generalized hostility, vilification of the human.
8. *Projectivity.* Disposition to believe that wild and dangerous things go on in the world; the projection outward of unconscious emotional impulses.
9. *Sex.* Ego-alien sexuality; exaggerated concern with sexual "goings on," and punitiveness toward violators of sex mores.

Although the subparts of the complex may be specified in this fashion, they actually are considered closely cohering parts of one syndrome. The above nine "hypothetical clusters" of authoritarianism are derived from clinical observations and interviews. Each item of the F scale supposedly measures one or more of these facets of authoritarianism. Because of heavy reliance on this scale among the original authors and subsequent researchers, this instrument is, in large part, the working definition of authoritarianism.

The study of authoritarianism, as initiated by the group at Berkeley, had great impact on social psychology for many reasons. First, the researchers sought to establish connections among diverse expressed opinions by showing a common core of psychological meaning. Functionally, the various opinions were held to be related to prejudice. Second, they developed a general theoretical framework to explain the sources of these attitudes. Third, they formulated a measuring scale which found ready application in a wide variety of research efforts—from large-scale political surveys to small group experiments. For these as well as other reasons, the study of authoritarianism attracted much interest.

II. SOME CRITICISMS OF *THE AUTHORITARIAN PERSONALITY*

Since its publication, a number of scholars have examined in detail *The Authoritarian Personality*. Hyman and Sheatsley (1954) all but demolished the work with their incisive critique. They concerned themselves specifically with questions of populations, sampling, measuring instruments, and analyses in the Berkeley investigations. Evaluating the data as related to the guiding framework advanced by Adorno and his colleagues, Hyman and Sheatsley found serious shortcomings: the samples were not representative, the wedding of survey and intensive clinical methods did not make use of the merits of each, statistics and analyses proved weak and inaccurate, the variable of formal education in the samples was not controlled, and alternative explanations were not examined. Most scathing of all are Hyman and Sheatsley's observations that the cumulative effects of the study's shortcomings "uniformly operate *in favor* of the authors' assumptions" (p. 121, italics in original), giving the impression of confirming the theory. Perhaps in response to these comments, Sanford (1956) answered that no systematic theory guided the research and that because of the evolving nature of the ideas and research, the authors often had to offer *ad hoc* explanations of their findings.

Research reported in *The Authoritarian Personality* clearly will not withstand evaluation on the basis that the studies flowed from systematic theory. Considering methodological shortcomings, the data have questionable relevance to the theory. Because there was criterion contamination, we cannot conclude that the interview material collected in the original studies supports the questionnaire results and hence the theory. The insight which promoted the work, however, is not minimized by the procedural inadequacies, and it is perhaps this insight which stimulated the flood of further studies on authoritarianism.

In his text on *Social Psychology*, Asch (1952) included a critique of *The Authoritarian Personality* which has received little attention, though it raises problems yet to be resolved satisfactorily. First, Asch rejected "the assumption that one can deduce the content of psychological processes from the content of attitude items" (p. 545). The correlations among the scales may represent simply a "lack of discrimination" by the respondent. In forcing a response to a test item, the investigator ordinarily has no information on the significance of an item's content to the respondent. In fact, Asch suggested that the responses obtained represented "global antipathy to anything strange" and lack of definite social sentiments rather than a well-articulated belief system. The role of *a* belief system has been a persistent problem in the study of authoritarianism. Second, in conceptualizing a relationship between personality and the social structure, the investigators ignored the role of structural variables in forming personality. This latter criticism recently has received more attention.

Asch's comments were supported by the conclusions Titus and Hollander (1957) reached in their review of research on the F scale. After examining studies of ideology, personality, and interpersonal behavior using the F scale, Titus and Hollander concluded that the "F scale correlates most sys-

8

tematically with other paper-and-pencil measu
systematically with interpersonal behaviors, pa
situational conditions are varied" (p. 62).

Several investigators have tried to develop
explanations for authoritarianism. For example, St\   ...ud
Hoult (1959) found an approach to authoritarianism in the
individual's skill at mastering roles, both in taking on various
roles and in playing roles appropriately. While regarding
restricted role mastery as characteristic of an authoritarian
family background, they also recognized the effect of other
social factors on role behavior—degree of education, age,
restrictiveness of environment, and minority group membership. Thus, situational structural contributions to authoritarianism are recognized explicitly, and the impact of family
and childhood experiences are kept in the explanation but in
an extended framework. Cumming and Henry (1961) have
taken steps toward testing this approach by empirical
research.

Kelman and Barclay (1963) have suggested a consideration of psychological and sociocultural conditions in
interpreting F scale scores. According to their view,
authoritarianism is a joint function of a person's psychological predispositions (capacity) and the experience provided by his environment. "A low scorer is a person whose
psychological universe is relatively wide. He sees events in
a variety of contexts. He is aware of the existence of a range
of customs, values, and approaches to life. He expects
differences between people and is tolerant of them. A high
scorer, by contrast, is a person who moves in very narrow
circles. He sees events only in the context of his own
limited frame of reference. He does not recognize the existence of a range of values and approaches, and is intolerant
of differences" (p. 608). Kelman and Barclay cited well-
documented findings that higher F scale scores relate to

9

lower intelligence, less education and similar factors and offered further data of their own.

Do authoritarian-related attitudes expressed by individuals of different intellectual levels reflect similar personality processes? According to one writer (Simon, 1965), the authoritarian personality arises from emotional immaturity and is manifested in a "quest for subjective certainty." Simon distinguished emotional maturity from intellectual competence. Even though the emotionally immature and the intellectually inept may respond similarly in certain situations, he believed their long-range behavior to be quite different. Simon's comments raised a genuine problem related, of course, to the comments of Asch and the interpretation given to responses on the F scale by those with little education or sophistication. While Simon's discussion is valuable in posing the problem, he offered neither data nor specific suggestions for instruments which could test the different variables he theorized were involved.

With reference to the content of authoritarian attitudes, it is now commonly accepted that *The Authoritarian Personality* dealt principally with conservative ideology, since the F scale measures authoritarianism of the political right. In his essay on the right and the left in politics, Shils (1954) argued that the F scale taps only the political right. Further, he showed the similarity of qualities of the left and right in existing sociopolitical systems, drawing parallels between communism and fascism. In his view the so-called rigid low scorers on the F scale (regarded as nonauthoritarians) could be viewed as authoritarians of the left. In this same vein, Christie (in Christie and Jahoda, 1954) cited evidence from the Berkeley studies which indicated that authoritarians of the left would not score high on the F scale. Barker (1963) recently offered evidence supporting this point.

INTRODUCTION

To correct these conceptual biases Rokeach (1960) developed the theory of dogmatism as part of his interpretation and extension of authoritarianism. He regarded dogmatism as a characteristic of individual cognitive structure, not tied to a specific ideology. What is crucial, according to Rokeach, is the tenacity with which beliefs are held, not the beliefs themselves. A high degree of dogmatism appears in the form of (a) sharp distinctions between beliefs and disbeliefs, the existence of contradictory beliefs, and little differentiation among disbeliefs; (b) a basic outlook of pessimism, fear, and concern with power; and (c) a belief in the absolute nature of authority, intolerance of anyone who disagrees, and "party-line" thinking. According to Rokeach, these characteristics form a core to which a variety of peripheral beliefs can be attached.

To support his thesis of cognitive structure, Rokeach developed scales of dogmatism and opinionation. These scales have had varied application, yielding evidence that his conceptualization is more widely applicable than that of the F scale. Some of the results, although based on few cases, effectively differentiated between general authoritarianism and the ideology of the extreme right.

Although promising in its theoretical distinctiveness, principally the emphasis on cognitive structure, Rokeach's approach encounters some difficulty at the empirical level. One criticism is that the dogmatism scale is constructed, as is the F scale, with all items worded in the direction of dogmatism. This makes the scale liable to the same response bias problems as the F scale, discussed in a subsequent section.

A second empirical difficulty is that the D scale is rather highly correlated with the F scale (with correlations ranging from .54 to .77) to support the distinctions between the two.

Using the correlation between F and D for their combined sample from Kerlinger and Rokeach (1966) and adjusting it for the unreliability of the scales, we obtained a true score correlation of .88. Kerlinger and Rokeach offered factorial evidence on the proposition that items from the F and D scale are distinct. A dogmatism factor and two mixed factors (containing both F and D items at the first-order factor level) constitute their second-order factors. They cite in a footnote (p. 395) two other analyses they performed that support the distinguishability of F and D scale items. Their findings indicate, however, considerable overlap in the factorial structure of the two scales.

In *The Open and Closed Mind* Rokeach and his coworkers touched on a variety of topics, including problem-solving, perception, prejudice, the creation of dogma, and changes in values. The scope of their work is both a strength and a weakness. On one hand, application of the dogmatism concept to a wide variety of phenomena is challenging and suggestive of many hypotheses; on the other hand, the data offered to support any one application of the theory are not strong. There are plausible alternative explanations for many of the findings. In addition, the heavy (but not unusual) reliance placed on "samples" of student groups makes generalization of the findings problematic. Finally, the relationship of the concept of dogmatism to that of authoritarianism, as developed by Adorno and his coworkers needs further clarification (see Rokeach, 1961), even though Rokeach apparently accepted the developmental account given by the Berkeley group. Specifically, can the psychoanalytic language of the Berkeley formulation be translated directly into Rokeach's "cognitive" account ("genotypic" similarity), and can all expressions of authoritarianism be subsumed under the more general expression of dogmatism ("phenotypic" similarity)?

INTRODUCTION

III. THE PROBLEM OF RESPONSE BIAS

Much concern has been given to the role of response bias or acquiescence* in determining F scale scores. A response bias occurs when a respondent selects certain categories of responses regardless of question content (e.g., selects the "agree" category) or systematically distorts his responses as a function of the content (e.g., picks the socially desirable response). Studies to date do not determine the degree to which these biases independently affect F scale scores, though the distinction is theoretically and methodologically important. Bias can affect the F scale because in its original form all items are worded so that agreement uniformly indicates authoritarianism. General tendencies exist to agree or to answer "true" on paper-and-pencil tests (e.g., Cronbach, 1946). When the test score is to some degree determined by such a response bias, interpretation based on content becomes questionable. We will refer to this type of response bias as "acquiescence." An early review (Smith, 1950) foreshadowed concern with this issue in interpretation of F scale scores.

Several investigators have examined the influence of this bias on F scale scores, using two basic strategies. One approach to the problem independently measures acquiescence, typically the number of "true," "yes," or "agree" responses to items covering a wide variety of content. Sometimes tests include difficult material to reduce the probability that a respondent knows the correct responses to all items; sometimes apparently factual items are fictitious. A high score thus indicates a tendency to agree with test items, and

---

* The general terms "response bias" or "acquiescence" will be used to avoid the specific implications of "set" or "style." These distinctions are discussed subsequently. The lack of a standardized meaning in the literature for these terms is awkward, but hardly atypical for social science (see Rorer, 1965).

if scores on such measures correlate highly with F scale scores, the implication is that acquiescence tendencies are contaminating authoritarianism scores. This approach assumes that the only cause of covariation in scores on the F scale and the measure of acquiescence is the predisposition to agree. Any other factor that may contribute to a correlation between the F scale and the acquiescence measure (e.g., the possibility that those who freely endorse broad negative generalizations about people are less well informed, therefore tending to answer "true" or "agree" to a difficult information test) is assumed to be inoperative. This assumption often is not valid. (See discussion by Rorer, 1965).

The evidence of acquiescence tendencies contaminating F scale scores is not consistent. For example, a scale composed of 33 MMPI items with diverse content, when scored for the number of "true" responses ("plus" scale), yielded moderate positive relationships to F scale scores (Cohn, 1953; Gage, Leavitt, and Stone, 1957). Couch and Keniston (1960) reported a correlation of .37 between scores on a factorially derived F scale and an "Overall Agreement Score," developed from "agree" responses to items with diverse content. In a second study, however, there was no relationship between the F measure and a shortened form of the agreement test. Shelly (1956) found a barely significant correlation between antisemitism scores (one of the early scales leading to, and closely related to, the F scale) and "like much" responses to the Berg and Hunt Perceptual Reaction Test. While these results indicated some support for the acquiescence interpretation, they are tempered by the fact that a very low relationship was later obtained between two different measures of acquiescence used by Gage, Leavitt, and Stone (1957). Perhaps these measures

14

tapped different aspects of acquiescence; perhaps no simple interpretation of acquiescence is tenable.

Carey, Rogow, and Farrell (1957) argued that scores on the F scale reflect "agreement with values expressed in an authoritarian manner" and do not depend upon the content of those values. They constructed two sets of aphorisms, one expressing democratic ideals and the other expressing antidemocratic ideals. Both scales, when scored for *agreement* with the statement and frequency of personal usage reported by the subject, showed positive relationships with the F scale. The consistency in responses over the three scales, then, may be explained by the tendency to agree.

In a penetrating discussion of response bias Rorer (1965) questioned the significance of evidence on acquiescence. He argued that if the results are to be attributed to response bias, covariation due to content similarities must be eliminated. Such similarities, due to item form and content, he said, are more pervasive than heretofore recognized. Finally, he pointed out that scores on scales designed to measure agreement response styles themselves intercorrelate only slightly (as in the Gage, Leavitt, and Stone study), which raises questions about what variables these scales actually are measuring. His discussion suggested the inadequacy of the evidence on response bias (i.e., a content-free way of responding) as a significant factor in interpreting the F scale.

A second strategy for adducing evidence on response bias appears in studies in which the wording of F scale items is reversed. Rewriting the "positively" worded items negatively, however, is a difficult task. Consider the following item from the scale: "Most people don't realize how much our lives are controlled by plots hatched in secret places." Ideally, a reversal would embody an equally strong statement of an opposite nonauthoritarian attitude. But, would

15

it concern *how much people realize* (e.g., "most people *do* realize how much our lives are controlled by plots hatched in secret places"); or, the amount of control (e.g., "most people don't realize how *little* our lives are controlled by plots hatched in secret places"); or the means of achieving decisions (e.g., "most people don't realize how much our lives are controlled by *decisions reached in public debate"*); or other phrasing? Matters of logical reversals, psychological reversals, and item style and extremity are important in this strategy of studying response bias in the F scale, and researchers have used various types of reversals (see, for example, discussion by Christie and others, 1958).

One kind of evidence on response bias offered by these studies is the correlation between scores on authoritarianism from the original scale and from a scale made up of reversed items. If reversals are adequate, the latter constitutes an equivalent form of the scale. Lack of correspondence between sets of scores obtained from the separate scales supposedly indicates response set, although a major assumption here is "other things being equal." A second common difficulty here is low reliability of reversed scales.

Studies using positive and negative forms of the F scale (or similar measures) have not solved the response bias problem. Some studies yielded evidence that content is important in responses to the F scale as reversed items appeared to measure more or less the same thing as the original items (Bass, 1955; Schulberg, 1961). Couch and Keniston (1960), using new F negative items designed to appeal to nonauthoritarians, found a correlation of minus .70 between the positive and negative versions. Chapman and Campbell (1959) found a correlation of .29 between positive and negative versions of the F scale (both scored for authoritarianism); comparing this to a theoretical expectation of .54, they attributed the difference to response bias. Influences other than response bias, however, could account for the attenuated relationship (Christie and others, 1958).

Other studies using positive and negative item formats obtained conflicting results, no relationship, or results which indicated that those who appeared authoritarian on one measure were nonauthoritarian on the other. Chapman and Campbell (1957) found correlations of .17 and minus .01 between original and reversed F scale items in two studies with analysis of the reversed items showing a wide range of relationships to the original items. However, little relationship between original and reversed scales was reported by Foster and Gregg (1963) and by Jackson and Messick (1957). The latter study used positively worded Ethnocentrism Scale items and a reversed F scale. Using five different subject groups, Leavitt, Hax, and Roche (1955) found in four groups low to moderate relationships. For the fifth group high scores on the original scale were associated with low scores on the reversed scale. An analysis of the high and low scorers suggested that low scorers on the original F scale responded more to content than did high scorers.

Evidence most suggestive of a response bias came from a study by Jackson, Messick, and Solley (1957). They found a significant relationship opposite to that which would be expected on the basis of content. Campbell, Converse, Miller, and Stokes (1960) obtained a similar result with five F positive and five F negative items administered to a national sample.

Another approach to the problem of response bias in the F scale considers authoritarianism as measured by item content (balanced by item wording) and acquiescence as measured by "agree" responses, deriving scores from both original and reversed F scale items. Several studies offer evidence on the relationship between the content of F scale items and acquiescence. Messick and Frederiksen (1958), using a scale composed of 15 original and 15 reversed items, derived an authoritarianism score and a response set score, both of which had rather low reliability (split half). There was no relationship between these two variables. The authors suggested that the low content reliability is due to the complex nature of authoritarianism, conceived to be a set of traits. Eysenck (1962) analyzed content and response bias scores from a balanced form of the F scale (Jackson and Messick, 1957), along with scores from several personality measures such as his extraversion and neuroticism scales. The subjects were 137 neurotic inpatients in two British hospitals. He identified four factors, the third of which he called "antifascist" by virtue of a high loading on authoritarianism of minus .52; the measure of acquiescence from the authoritarianism scale loaded minus .02 on this factor. The fourth factor was labeled acquiescence response set, with a loading of .96 for the acquiescence score from the F scale. The content score loaded .30 on this dimension. Eysenck concluded that acquiescence may be peculiar to questionnaires concerning attitudes and opinions.

Chapman and Bock (1958) calculated the percentages of variance attributable to content, acquiescence, and covariance between the two factors. The authors analyzed previously published work, finding that about 30-40 percent of the total variance in F scale scores may be ascribed to content with the remainder of the reliable variance (30-40 percent of the total) divided between acquiescence and content-set covariance.

Peabody (1964) has criticized the model used by Chapman and Bock and that proposed by Messick and Frederiksen (1958; see also Messick, 1961) as inappropriate to testing content and response bias variance in F scale scores and proposed an alternative procedure. Peabody's proposal for dealing with the problem involved a combination of both plus and minus response versions of the same items (see discussion of Peabody, 1961, below) and the adjustment of procontent and anticontent responses by a factor intended to represent the set contribution to these apparently content-determined responses. Using his method, Peabody found the relative contribution of set and content to be of the order of 3:1. This estimate is based on data from American and English engineering students, the same data reported in Peabody (1961).

Using a carefully worked-out design, Peabody (1961) attempted to find the degree of acquiescence in the F, dogmatism, antisemitism, and (his own) conservatism scales. For each of the four scales, he constructed a reversed version: for example, he used 28 items from the positively worded F scale and 28 reversed, or negative, items developed according to psychological meaningfulness. He split both the positive and negative versions of each scale into halves. The respondents completed half of each scale at one session and the other half at a second session. Peabody defined a consistent response as either agreement with the positively worded item and disagreement with its reversal, or disagreement with the positively worded item and agreement with the reversal. Agreement or disagreement with both versions supposedly indicated the absence of the belief in the subject's value system (or, at least, some kind of variance making it impossible to place the respondent on the content dimension).

Based on two different groups of engineering students (one in the United States and one in England), the results were quite similar for both the F and the dogmatism scales. First, 30-35 percent of the responses amounted to double agreements; consistently authoritarian responses were infrequent (14-16 percent); the nonauthoritarian pattern was the most consistent (42-47 percent). Second, correlations between the positive and negative versions were low (minus .18 for the F scale and minus .36 for the dogmatism scale with the negative versions scored for low authoritarianism and low dogmatism). Peabody also found moderate to high correlations among positive versions of the F, dogmatism, and antisemitism scales and attributed these relationships to a combination of nonauthoritarian attitudes and agreement response set. In his discussion, he raised the question of serious misrepresentation of respondents who do not have the attitudes indicated by responses to "plus" versions of the scales (see also Peabody 1966). Two factors in the study, however, limit the interpretation of results. First, the negative versions of the F and dogmatism scales typically exhibited low levels of reliability. Second, generalization of the percentages of responses falling into the different response types can only be hedged with caution since the results are based on groups of students.

Several studies now indicate the inaccuracy of referring to response bias in general in F scale scores. Peabody's design, for example, allowed comparison of respondents who were procontent (i.e., authoritarian), anticontent (i.e., nonauthoritarian), yeasayers, and naysayers. His data showed a minority of procontent subjects and a substantial majority of anticontent subjects. He also found a sizable percentage of yeasayers, but no naysayers. Since the yeasayers in his study had to be the high F subjects on the original scale, his data agreed nicely with the less direct evidence offered by Leavitt and his coworkers (1955) that there is great consistency in F positive and F negative scores for subjects who appear to be nonauthoritarian on the original scale. If scores on the F scale were affected by response set, then those who disagreed in some measure with the original items should have appeared as naysayers in comparisons between scores based on F positive and F negative items.

Peabody's conclusion that subjects scoring higher on the F scale displayed acquiescence rather than procontent (authoritarian) attitudes has been questioned by Samelson (1964), who proposed an alternative interpretation of Peabody's data. Where items and their reversals are dealt with dichotomously, the symmetry of the reversals as well as the direction of the wording must be considered in interpretation. Samelson's reanalysis showed that Peabody's results can be interpreted as influenced by asymmetric item reversals, discussed by Peabody from a different point of view.

As is the case in those studies which examine acquiescence in the F scale by correlations with agreement response scales and the like, the use of item reversals faces the criticism that their results were caused by content-related factors rather than acquiescence, social desirability, or some other response bias. If there had been no evidence of inconsistency between F positive and F negative items, the problem would have been simpler, even though the validity of the responses still could be questioned. But the problem is how to account for the obvious inconsistency of one form of the scale with the other, which cannot be accounted for on such psychometric grounds as the low reliabilities for reversed scales. Most investigators assumed that inconsistency in responses was prima facie evidence for response bias. Life, it appears, is more complex. Rorer detailed some of this complexity. So did Rokeach (1963), specifically with respect to the double agreement issue, inferred from studies of reversed scales, but tested only in studies employing a design like that of Peabody. The same problems of interpretation apply to the dogmatism scale. Rokeach discusses the response set problem in his book and concludes that it really is not a problem (1960). As noted in Smith's review

(1960), the evidence is not entirely convincing. Direct evidence that the dogmatism measure is liable to acquiescence is reported by Lichtenstein, Quinn, and Hover (1961).

Rokeach asserted that in addition to response bias, two content-related factors could account for double agreements (and presumably the findings with reversed items). The first possibility is that those with profascist tendencies agreed with F positive items because such items represent their true beliefs, and with F negative items because it was the socially appropriate thing to do, even though they did not possess the corresponding beliefs. By this hypothesis, double agreements indicated pro-authoritarian tendencies rather than acquiescent response bias. This interpretation was challenged by Peabody (1966) who asserted that in the absence of supporting data there is no compelling reason to interpret double agreements as authoritarianism.*

Further, Peabody cited a study by Stanley and Martin (1964) that found no correlation between social desirability and lie scales, on one hand, and a reversed dogmatism scale on the other. More important evidence on this question in the Stanley and Martin study was the significant negative correlation (minus .234) between the dogmatism scale and the social desirability scale: those higher on dogmatism gave less socially desirable responses. However, the analyses performed by Stanley and Martin are largely irrelevant to the hypothesis suggested by Rokeach.

Rokeach's second hypothesis, again based on content, is that subjects actually tell the truth in both of the inconsistent responses, indicating inconsistent beliefs. Peabody (1966)

* On this point it is interesting to note that studies involving comparisons of F positive and reversed items typically examine patterns of groups dichotomized on the basis of responses to the original items, not the reversals. Such a procedure of course assumes that the original scale is somehow a better measure of authoritarianism.

replied that acceptance of this analysis destroys the notion that the F scale is a measure of authoritarianism—that Rokeach destroys what he seeks to preserve. However, Peabody's data show that this sort of inconsistency can reasonably be attributed to middle-scale respondents. Those in the middle of the scale should be the least certain, most ambivalent, or most indifferent, leading to more vacillation and greater acceptance of contradictory items. The argument that Peabody used would be more substantial if "highs" on the F scale—those who exhibit double agreement —were in fact high rather than midrange. But even then it would be meaningful to know to what extent compartmentalization, redefinition, and other forms of dealing with self-contradictory beliefs are used by those scoring high on the F positive items.

An additional point on response bias is that one of the nine hypothetical clusters constituting the concept of authoritarianism is "authoritarian submission" and has been interpreted as a tendency to acquiesce to authoritative, declarative statements. The F scale contains such statements, and in view of this, one might conclude that whatever response bias is included in F scale scores is appropriate.

Working with the premise that agreement is an aspect of authoritarianism, several investigators have concluded that use of F positive items enhances the discriminability or validity of the scale (Leavitt, Hax, and Roche, 1955; Gage, Leavitt, and Stone, 1957; Gage and Chattergee, 1960). These authors argued that because authoritarian submission is an integral part of authoritarianism, agreement with authoritarian content indicates authoritarianism both logically and psychologically. By their argument, agreement with an F negative item indicates logical nonauthoritarianism but psychological authoritarianism, since the response is one of agreement. Authoritarian submission, as reflected in acqui-escence to items, is in this view given singular importance. Gage, Leavitt, and Stone, and Gage and Chattergee offered evidence to show that items written so that agreement indicates content authoritarianism (like those on the F scale, but from the Minnesota Teacher Attitude Inventory) dis-criminate between teachers in their tendencies to behave in an authoritarian fashion (as rated by principals) better than items written so that agreement indicates nonauthori-tarianism.

Some other studies have reported that F positive items discriminate better than F negative items. This was the experience of Adorno and his associates in writing items for their scales. A difficulty with subsequent work correlating F positive and F negative items with an outside criterion is that the reversed items seldom show variances and reliabilities comparable to the originals.

Zuckerman and Eisen (1962) reported that authoritari-anism as measured by 15 original items correlated signifi-cantly (.48) with responses to an essay test on "current issues and personal values," scored for authoritarian and nonauthoritarian responses. Holding acquiescence constant by statistically partialing it out through use of scores on Bass' Famous Sayings test reduced the correlation to .39 (still significant). Fifteen negatively worded items taken from Christie and others failed to correlate with the criterion. The correlation between F positive scores and the Bass scale was .47; original and reversed F scale items correlated minus .41 with high scores on *both* scales indicating author-itarianism. Reliabilities of the positively-worded and nega-tively-worded scales were not given. As mentioned earlier, reversed F scales typically exhibit much lower (and often unacceptable) levels of reliability, reducing the possibility of their correlating with anything.

24

INTRODUCTION

Even after 15 years of research, the influence of acquiescence on scores from the F scale is difficult to assess. This is due in part to mechanical problems in isolating acquiescence, but it is also due to the likelihood that the interaction between acquiescence and authoritarianism is complex.

On one side of the authoritarianism-acquiescence dichotomy is the disposition to agree, which may be a personality trait or dimension. Rorer pointed out the low degree of intercorrelation among measures of acquiescence, and we cannot but agree that this challenges the conception of acquiescence as a unitary predisposition. Yet conceptually a dimension of acquiescence makes sense. Some empirical evidence for this view is found in the studies by Couch and Keniston (1960) and Smith (1965) who distinguish patterns of acquiescence (impulsiveness, susceptibility to stimuli, accepting) and authoritarianism (conventionality, overcontrol, rigidity, and premature closure).

Acquiescence effects work through interaction with statements on a scale, the outcome of which is a blending of at least two dispositions. These items can mediate the influence of the content dimension or response bias; in the present instance, authoritarianism or acquiescence. They can also affect the influence of actual knowledge as compared with disposition to agree in difficult information tests and might generate low relationships between scales designed to measure acquiescence by items of different form and content.

As seen from the studies reviewed, much of the evidence regarding acquiescence bias in F scale scores comes from studies in which investigators attempted to create opposites of original items. Serious questions concerning the adequacy of this tactic have been raised (Christie and others, 1958; Rorer, 1965). The lack of relationship between F positive and F negative items may reflect a great deal more than response bias.

The restricted range and lower reliabilities of the reversed scales are probably partially a result of midrange subjects' (the "authoritarians" in most studies) vacillation and indecision leading to agreement with the F negative items. The competing forces of set and content variables may account for many subjects who appear in the midrange on the reversed scale.

One sometimes-used and often-recommended means of reducing response bias is to balance the number of positive and negative items on the scale. This, however, does not solve the problem completely. If a disposition to agree influences response to items on a paper-and-pencil test, a balanced scale becomes a measure of relative strength of the dispositions to agree and to be authoritarian. Insofar as acquiescence determines responses to the negative items, for example, the score on authoritarianism goes down. And it is only the set-free respondent who can achieve the limiting score on authoritarianism. Another way of saying this is that while on the positively worded F scale high scores may be caused by either the disposition to agree or authoritarianism, on a balanced scale high scores on authoritarianism can occur only when there are no tendencies either to agree or disagree.

The disposition to agree may itself be a facet of authoritarianism. Agreement with things authoritative certainly is contained in the theory leading to the development of authoritarianism as a construct, including the cultural and international events that inspired the Berkeley studies. Because this is true, the decision of whether to use a balanced scale or a positively worded scale is even more difficult.

In view of bias problems, how are we to evaluate scores

on the F positive scale? Do scores result from response bias or authoritarianism or both? The data, even with their limitations, show there is considerably more consistency in correlations between positive and negative forms of the scale for subjects who score low on the original scale than for subjects who score high. The high scorers, in fact, appear to respond more in terms of agreement than of authoritarianism. The latter subjects on the scale are midrange or only slightly more authoritarian. And in terms of response to content, these subjects would be expected to be less certain and therefore more readily influenced by response bias. Subjects who score low on the original scale are not simply low in acquiescence, but are anticontent, demonstrated by their tendency to reject positive items and accept reversed items. Because midrange subjects will acquiesce to authoritarian statements, they score further toward the authoritarianism end of the scale than the "lows," but only to the extent that the low scores can be attributed to content rather than simply a naysaying response style (i.e., responding "no" or "disagree" regardless of content). The assertion in most studies that "highs" on the scale result from response bias is simply to say that these respondents are more midrange in authoritarianism and that no real "highs" have been identified. This thesis would be weakened if it were shown that respondents who agree highly with items on the F scale, say 5.0 or 5.5 and higher on the original 1-7 scale, also agree consistently with adequately-reversed anticontent items.

Are these "highs" then no more or less authoritarian than the lows on the scale and does their score pattern reflect agreement response in the absence of authoritarianism? It is possible that midrange scorers on the scale are more authoritarian than the low scorers, if only in their disposition to acquiesce to such items as make up the scale. This is not

27

merely agreement, but agreement with a certain content. Culturally, these subjects are more likely to be those who support social practices that maintain the status quo and punish deviants. However, they cannot be regarded as prototypic authoritarians or anything approaching the extreme caricature drawn by the language of the Berkeley studies. Doubtless, they do not have a well-developed ideology concerning power, politics, and people. More likely, they are unsettled or apathetic about these things. By this reasoning, then, the typical study compares subjects who are nonauthoritarian with those who are nonauthoritarian to slightly authoritarian. In Peabody's terminology, those with anticontent attitudes are compared with these who are neither anticontent nor procontent plus those who are slightly procontent.

Are correlations of scores on authoritarianism scales with other responses spurious? They may be, if the other scale contains a considerable response set component. If present estimates of acquiescence variance in the F scale, even considering the problems of their determination, are at all correct, then correlations with other scales in the neighborhood of .40 could be generated on the basis of response bias alone. If such a correlation were to be interpreted on the basis of acquiescence, however, it would be necessary to assume or demonstrate that the other scales contain substantial acquiescence variance or are highly correlated with acquiescence.

It is possible that the acquiescence variance in the F scale due to the influence of midrange subjects would promote correlations with other scales that do not contain response set variance, but correlate highly with acquiescence. But as Christie and his coworkers pointed out (1958), scores on the F scale have shown relationships to scores on variables not subject to response bias. This fact supports a content interpretation to the extent that the second variable can be demonstrated intuitively or empirically to be free from response bias.

Research and theory dealing with response bias is both complex and confusing, but some understanding of this contaminating factor is crucial for the interpretation of results of many studies. As we sifted through the research stemming from *The Authoritarian Personality*, the problem of response bias intruded frequently in evaluation. We believe results based on paper-and-pencil tests are ambiguous to the extent that the tests may evoke acquiescence. We discuss this ambiguity where it affects interpretations of studies. However, not all the research on authoritarianism involves paper-and-pencil tests, and not all such tests are liable to acquiescence response bias.

That branch of research dealing with response bias can easily lose sight of the theoretical nature of authoritarianism, and overemphasize the study of questionnaire responses while neglecting the implications of authoritarian style and content. Only rarely do investigators use an obvious source of information about the meaning of responses—the subjects themselves. It is as if reliance on properties of numbers, scoring, and correlation coefficients substitutes for probing beyond the checkmark on a paper-and-pencil test. At the least, the creation of new types and sources of measurement is required before many of the disputes over interpretation of responses to the F scale can be resolved.

IV. USE OF THE F SCALE: PROBLEMS
AND ALTERNATIVES

The various types of research done with the F scale illustrate the methodological armamentarium of the social psychologist. Personality assessment, survey methods, laboratory experiments, and other approaches have been employed. Each approach has inherent shortcomings, and in some cases these limitations pose difficulties in interpretation. There are some special problems in the numerous findings based on the F scale. One of these is response bias, reviewed in the previous section. It does not have clearcut status as a legitimate explanatory mechanism in the theory of authoritarianism. (The articles by Simon, 1954, and Blalock, 1961, are useful references in this connection.)

Response bias, often regarded as spuriousness, seems to vary in its effect with the nature of the sample. Apparently, the more the respondents represent the general population, the greater the problem of response bias. Restricting the nature of the sample used (if we can speak of a "sample" in most of the research on authoritarianism) does not solve the problem, because the correlates of acquiescence often are not psychological variables but are indicators of sophistication, richness of experience, or normative beliefs (education or socioeconomic status, for example). The known *psychological* correlates of acquiescence appear to have quite subtle effects (Quinn, 1963).

Using the F scale in a survey design has, in practice, an additional drawback. Typically, very short forms of the test are used (e.g., five-item versions) which cannot be evaluated the same as the original form(s) of the F scale.

In experimental work done with the F scale (or the dogmatism scale), authoritarianism is almost never a dependent variable; nor is it a true independent variable, because typically subjects are selected by extreme scores without random assignment or matching of subjects. However, if the experiments result in positive findings, either these findings are valid or else the method of selecting subjects confounds authoritarianism with other variables. If acquiescence, regarded as a separate dimension, is the disturbing factor, then the results on dependent variables not subject to acquiescence should at least show considerably different variance among the high and low scorers (on the F scale) since some subjects are erroneously called authoritarians. Otherwise, we must look for some other factors in the selection process which would account for differences on the dependent scores. Krug (1961) made a complementary point on the basis of factor analysis of F scale items; since his results indicated that the F scale was multidimensional, he concluded that a total F scale score obscured relationships which would be found with subsets of items.

Most of the research reviewed concerned one aspect of authoritarianism, such as rigidity in cognitive functioning, rejection of outgroups, or conformity to authority. The working definition employed in these studies, however, actually includes several different aspects of the concept. Classification on the basis of authoritarianism involves averaging the various dimension scores into an overall composite. That procedure resulted in loss of precision in measuring those authoritarian aspects of central interest to the investigator because subjects classified as authoritarian can include those scoring both high and low on a given dimension. Specifying and measuring significant parts of the concept and differentiating them from each other is a problem in such research.

Sampling procedures of *The Authoritarian Personality* were criticized by Hyman and Sheatsley (1954), who concluded that the results could not be generalized to any known population because of the unrepresentative respondents studied. That problem is still with us. Its crux is the use of college students for research samples. In some cases, students may serve appropriately as respondents; in most cases, the researcher intends to generalize his results to the adult population. The number of college students who have filled out one or more versions of the F scale must be astronomical, but the results are no closer to proper generalization than ten years ago. Surely, there must be some acceptable middle ground between the convenience and accessibility of students, and the cost and problems of sample surveys.

Because of F scale deficiencies investigators have sought alternatives to the original F scale as a measure of authoritarianism. Webster, Sanford, and Freedman (1955) designed a new instrument using true-false items selected for relationship to original F scale scores using responses of college freshmen. In their sample the correlation between F and the new scale was estimated to be .77. A subsequent study using this scale (Harvey, 1962) with a sample of undergraduate college students yielded a similar correlation of .72. Hites and Kellog (1964) reported a .66 correlation between F and the Webster, Sanford, and Freedman scale. The reliability coefficient of the new scale in the study by Webster and his colleagues was higher than .80 (Kruder-Richardson). Response bias is still a potential problem with this scale since in 138 of the 149 statements constituting the scale the answer "true" indicates authoritarianism.

Berkowitz and Wolkon (1964) developed a forced-choice form of the F scale using 25 items from the original F scale and the reversals from Bass (1955) and from Christie and others (1958). They constructed two forms of the test. With two samples of college students, reliabilities were .41, .59, .71, and .69. Correlations with the 25 original F scale items as a scale were .69, .74, .83, and .84. A 12-item short form yielded a reliability of .58 and correlated .77 with the 25-item scale. Vaughn and White (1966) used the scale in a study of conformity.

Smith (1965) used another scale to measure authoritarianism in studies of Peace Corps volunteers. The scale contained two versions of 100 items each with wording and direction of the items varied systematically to avoid response bias. In addition, one form contained "personality"

32

items of the MMPI and CPI type, while the other contained "ideology" items. Cluster analysis of the subscales led to rejection of the "personality" form of the instrument; an acquiescence score and an authoritarianism score were derived for the other form. Also used in the study was a "Levinson F scale," a 24-item scale made up of 12 original F scale items and 12 items from the Traditional Family Ideology scale (Levinson and Huffman, 1955). Derived F correlated .66 with the Levinson F scale; derived acquiescence correlated .41 with the Levinson F.

In the study by Smith, derived F received impressive validation by correlating with descriptive Q sort items corresponding well with the characterizations of authoritarianism in the work of Adorno and his associates. A shortcoming of this scale, however, is the complexity and advanced vocabulary of the items, which limit its usefulness.

Levinson and Huffman (1955) developed a measure of autocratic family ideology, labeled the Traditional Family Ideology (TFI) scale. Test items, taken largely from clinical interviews, covered five areas: conventionalism, authoritarian submission, exaggerated masculinity and femininity, extreme emphasis on discipline, and moralistic rejection of impulse life. On the basis of data gathered from 42 women and 67 men who were night school college students, the authors reported a correlation of .73 with a 10-item version of the original F scale. The meaning of this correlation is not clear as 34 of the TFI items were written so that agreement indicated autocratic beliefs. This raises serious questions about acquiescence. The authors presented a short form of the TFI along with "validation" data, but all of the short form items were subject to potential response bias.

Many variations of the original F scale have been used. It is not uncommon for investigators to use some but not all of the items from the original scale. Other studies have used balanced scales made up of negatively worded items written specifically for the study or taken from earlier research. Christie and others (1958) and Bass (1955) reversals have had wide use. Rokeach's dogmatism scale not only is a major revision of the F scale but is also a new conceptualization of authoritarianism.

Excepting the scale used by Smith and the forced-choice forms developed by Berkowitz and Wolkon (1964), these revisions contain potential response bias. Selection of items or specific dimensions derived from theory would be an alternative approach to scales assessing general authoritarianism. A few carefully chosen and scaled items dealing, for example, with distrust of people might yield more meaningful results (see Messick and Jackson, 1958). Whatever course is chosen, the investigator no longer can ignore the shortcomings inherent in F scale scores.

Social Characteristics
and Authoritarianism

Investigators have focused considerable attention on the relationship of authoritarianism and various social variables, including social groupings and demographic characteristics. They have regarded education, in particular, as an important influence on F scale scores. Although the *Authoritarian Personality* study did use survey methods, it did not examine authoritarianism within a representative population (Hyman and Sheatsley, 1954), nor did it contrast systematically subgroups of the population. It remained the task of later studies, some of which we will discuss, to explore the association between the F scale and social and cultural characteristics.

Some cross-cultural testing of the F scale has been made, as well as testing, within subcultural groups. Typically, respondents from cultural backgrounds reflecting a more overtly authoritarian style of life or more limited social perspectives yield higher F scale or dogmatism scores. For example, workers in Germany (Cohn and Carsch, 1954), and students in Near East countries (Prothro and Melikian,

1953) scored comparatively high on authoritarianism. Pettigrew (1958), however, reported that F scale responses of a large group of South African students were very similar to those of American students. In a survey study comparing a sample of union members in the United States with a sample of lower class respondents in Italy, Rose (1966) found a high level of authoritarianism in the Italian group. However, he questioned the validity of the instrument across cultures.

Using a Japanese translation of the Christie F scale items (including reversed items), Niyekawa (1960) compared responses of high school students in Japan with those of American students. Greater acquiescence and more extreme responses, regardless of direction, were evident in the Japanese sample. In addition, Japanese subjects from lower class and rural backgrounds scored higher on both authoritarianism and acquiescence; females were higher than males on authoritarianism, but not on acquiescence. Included among the measures were ratings on "authoritarianism" in family relationships. Rural students yielded higher scores on that measure, but there was no direct relationship between these ratings and subjects' scores on authoritarianism. According to the author, the pattern of relationships found in this study suggested that the assimilation of Western ideology had different effects on various strata in a society where leaders previously were quite "authoritarian."

Cross-cultural studies of social distance by Triandis and his coworkers (Triandis, Davis, and Takezawa, 1965) focused on patterns of acceptance or rejection of (hypothetical) persons with various characteristics and on some of the correlates of individual differences in discrimination. Theoretically the researchers regarded social discrimination as a product of cultural norms and personality. The research problem involved determining the relative importance of various factors (such as race) in different cultures and more or less universal personality dispositions related to social distance. Scales of social distance were standardized independently in Japan, Germany, and the United States. The subjects in each country (high school and college students) then evaluated hypothetical persons described with respect to race, occupation, religion, and nationality, with these descriptions systematically varied. Other measures were used, including both positive and negative F scale scores; the scores on authoritarianism were corrected for response bias. These investigators found that authoritarianism is related moderately to social distance in all three cultures. A picture of the characteristics of the universal ethnocentric person emerged from these results: he is authoritarian, conforming, uncritical of cultural values, conservative, and intolerant of ambiguity.

Many studies have linked authoritarianism and subcultural characteristics. Within the United States, higher scores on measures of authoritarianism typically came from those with more limited cultural backgrounds. Catholics (Brown and Brstryn, 1956; Rokeach, 1960) and Negroes (Smith and Prothro, 1957; Steckler, 1957; Kelman and Barclay, 1963), for example, registered high scores.

Attempts to measure systematically the relationship between authoritarianism and social status have been made. Several investigators found an inverse relationship between social class and F scale scores (Srole, 1956; Roberts and Rokeach, 1956; MacKinnon and Centers, 1956a; McDill, 1961). Occupational categories were used in the study by MacKinnon and Centers (1956a); in their results, there was an exception in the otherwise regular negative relationship between authoritarianism and occupational status: the white-collar group showed a higher percentage of respondents

37

with high scores on the F scale than did the manually skilled group (even though the manual group as a whole was higher in authoritarianism than other groups). Relevant here are the findings by Gurin, Veroff, and Feld (1960) that the white-collar group tends to be relatively high in frustration. Of interest also is the finding by MacKinnon and Centers that the weaker the self-identification with a social class, the smaller the percentage of high scorers on authoritarianism.

Lower socioeconomic groups may be more subject to "feelings of alienation" from others. Srole (1956) hypothesized that subjective "anomia" (feelings of helplessness) would be related to rejection of outgroups and to general authoritarianism. His definition of anomia included belief in indifference of community leaders to the individual's needs, the unpredictable nature of the social order, the meaninglessness of life to the individual, lack of trust in others, and the belief that social conditions were becoming worse. He found a greater degree of anomia was associated with lower socioeconomic status. This finding has been twice replicated, using the same scale (McDill, 1961; Roberts and Rokeach, 1956).

Campbell, Gurin, and Miller (1956) linked low socioeconomic status (less income, less education, lower occupational status) with low sense of political effectiveness. Stouffer (1955) found lower socioeconomic status respondents less liberal on questions of civil liberties. He found that those with low education were more intolerant on civil rights questions. Martin and Westie (1959) also observed more ethnic intolerance among those with lower occupational status and little education. In their study, the more prejudiced subjects also scored higher on a version of the F scale.

Some of these studies, however, included potential response bias as most items were worded so that agreement indicated intolerance, anomia, or the other variables tested. Probably some of the responses were due to the tendency of relatively unsophisticated subjects to respond favorably to "high-sounding aphorisms."

Even considering this possible contamination, is there evidence of greater "genuine" authoritarianism among people of lower status? Lipset (1959; 1960) cited survey evidence from the United States and other countries indicating the lower classes were less committed than the higher socio-economic classes to democratic norms. Although other factors in a given situation may override these tendencies, Lipset argued that authoritarianism is more "natural" to the condition of lower classes. He noted that these persons often prefer extreme movements urging quick and facile solutions to social problems and are characterized by rigidity of outlook based on impoverished experience and surroundings and by lack of education. Lipsitz (1965) found that data from three opinion surveys, containing a variety of items thought to reflect authoritarianism, bore out Lipset's contention. There were inconsistencies, and only those items which are most like F scale content showed a clearcut effect. However, Miller and Riessman (1961) took detailed exception to Lipset's conclusions.

Stember (1961), in explaining his findings that the highly educated show more prejudice in certain areas, suggested that the educated have many more contacts with current cultural thought and may respond to new, extreme fashions in the thoughts of an articulate elite. It may be that the distribution of preference for, and access to, extreme movements differs among various social groups and acts as a buffer against radical changes in the direction of authoritarian thought.

Sophistication apparently is another influence on F scale scores. Generally, more sophisticated respondents are less likely to endorse items such as those on the F scale. When the sample tested is more or less representative, authoritarianism as measured by the F scale shows a moderate negative relationship to education (MacKinnon and Centers, 1956a; Srole, 1956; Roberts and Rokeach, 1956; McDill, 1961). Christie estimated that the correlation would be minus .50 to minus .60 for the population (in Christie and Jahoda, 1954). He reported a national survey carried out by NORC which found a correlation of minus .54 between education and a form of F scale. In a survey on political attitudes, Campbell and others (1960), using a short but balanced (both positive and negative items) version of the F scale also found a correlation between these scores and educational level. In the data cited by Lipsitz (1965) relationships between social class and authoritarian responses diminished sharply when education was controlled.

In Stember's (1961) analysis of surveys on prejudice he treated educational level as the major independent variable. Depending on the question asked, education showed a variety of relationships to aspects of prejudice. The more educated were less likely to hold traditional stereotypes; they did not approve discriminatory policy or laws, or reject casual contacts. Yet, they were more likely to hold certain other stereotypes, to favor informal discrimination in some areas, and to reject intimate contacts. Furthermore, the effects of education in reducing prejudice proved strongest among those of lower social status. Hence, the impact of education on prejudice was complex. Stember pointed out that the way in which questions are phrased is important. Crudely worded items may bypass the educated, which is why "results of questions expressing extreme positions . . . have so often indicated a negative relationship between prejudice and education. When the issues are posed in more neutral terminology, no such relationship is evidenced" (p. 170).

Social characteristics such as those described above became meaningful only in relation to some theoretical structure explaining links between personality and membership in some social classification, as, for example, an age group. Class, education, occupation, religious group, and many other categories are interrelated. To what extent, for example, can amount of education account for the findings reviewed above? Through what mechanisms does it operate and at what level? The same questions can be asked in consideration of other background variables.

The variable of sophistication also relates closely to the problem of response bias. Discovery of an inverse relation between education and F scale scores can be taken at face value only if the F scale is a reasonably valid measure. But, the danger of content contamination by agreement response bias cannot be overlooked, so the meaning of different responses by educational level is ambiguous. However, related findings on alienation and intolerance support the likelihood of more authoritarian beliefs at lower social and educational levels. Beyond this, the salience of authoritarian attitudes in various groupings is an open question. (Cp. Stewart and Hoult, 1959; Cumming and Henry, 1961; Kelman and Barclay, 1963.)

Relationships between *rejection* of extreme-sounding statements and "sophistication," education, or related measures also have been theorized. Such a view complements the assertion that those "high" in authoritarianism tend to agree with lofty aphorisms.

Personality Characteristics
and Authoritarianism

Investigators have explored the relationship of authoritarianism to certain psychological variables, including aspects of cognitive functioning (especially rigidity and intolerance of ambiguity), psychopathology, anxiety, and prejudice. Although it is difficult to distinguish clearly between personality and social psychological variables (such as attitudes and values), we will discuss in this section studies focusing on persistent, stylistic aspects of behavior. We will also consider studies of dogmatism and the relationship of this concept to anxiety. Because of their special relationship to the beginnings of authoritarianism as a discrete field of study, we will cover studies of ethnic prejudice separately.

I. COGNITIVE FUNCTIONING

An important feature of authoritarianism according to Adorno and others (1950) is rigidity in thinking. Researchers have given that aspect of authoritarianism a great deal of attention with mixed success in outcome. In theoretical assertions investigators have expected those scoring high on the F scale to function less effectively in situations where cognitive shifts were required, to be intolerant of ambiguous situations, and to be less discriminating in their reactions to novel material. Upon closer examination, the set of appropriate research questions in these areas turns out to be quite complex. For example, cognitive rigidity and intolerance of cognitive ambiguity can be two quite different things.

One line of research involved the study of relationships between the F scale and inability to shift from an established "set" in solving a numerical problem (the Luchins' water jar problems). Originally, Rokeach (1948) found a positive relationship; Brown (1953), however, reported that the relationship held only when subjects were ego-involved. In 1955, French not only was unable to repeat Brown's results, but he also found no relationship of F scale scores to seven assorted measures of rigidity, including the water jar problems. While Jackson, Messick, and Solley (1957) did find an association, they also administered a reversed F scale and interpreted their results as reflecting acquiescence both in (original) F scale scores and responses to the measure of rigidity. To complete the picture, Levitt and Zuckerman (1959) after reviewing some 30 studies using the water jar problems as a measure of rigidity, concluded that "the water jar test is invalid as a measure of rigidity, and it has serious psychometric shortcomings no matter what it may be measuring" (p. 379).

Nor have studies using paper-and-pencil measures of intolerance of ambiguity fared much better (Davids, 1956; Kenny and Ginsberg, 1958). Millon (1957), however, differentiated between intolerance of ambiguity and rigidity in a novel perceptual task (autokinetic effect), finding that, among high scorers on the F scale, fewer trials were required to establish a norm in the perceived movement of the light. In addition, under conditions of high involvement the authoritarian subjects resisted change under conditions which ordinarily produce change; this result was interpreted as indicating rigidity.

Harvey and Caldwell (1959), studying judgment of distance between two briefly exposed lights, found a negative correlation (minus .436) between F scale scores and the extent to which a new distance greater than the first changed subsequent estimates of the initial distance. The authors interpret this finding as showing that authoritarianism promotes greater resistance to changing established concepts. Mischel and Schopler (1959) found that their student subjects who changed their prediction that the United States would reach the moon first to the prediction that Russia would reach the moon first were significantly less authoritarian as measured by the F scale than those who still maintained that the United States would beat Russia to the moon. The first prediction was made shortly after Sputnik I and the second just after Sputnik II.

Restle, Andrews, and Rokeach (1964) reported a difference between more and less dogmatic subjects on reversal learning and oddities problems. On oddities problems those with lower dogmatism scores performed better, reflecting their ability to grasp the principle involved. Reversal learning problems were interpreted as a task dependent on the experimenter's "authority." The authors claimed that closed-minded subjects performed better, even though the data were equivocal.

Studies of the differential effect of high and low authoritarianism as measured by the F and dogmatism scales in judging the favorableness of statements about social objects have suggested that only in the case of high relevance (or extreme ego-involvement) do these variables affect judgments. White, Alter, and Rardin (1965) predicted and obtained such results for those above the seventy-fifth percentile on both the F and dogmatism scales compared with those below the twenty-fifth percentile, but only in the case of judging statements about social acts (considered by the investigators to be motivationally relevant to the authoritarianism syndrome) and not in the case of judgments about prestige of occupations (considered not motivationally relevant). However, White and Harvey (1965) reported no relationship between F and dogmatism scale scores, and use of extreme categories, number of categories used, category width, and creation of new items in a judgment task that presumably should have been ego-involving. Judges were students at the University of Utah and members of the Mormon Church judging statements about their church. A measure of concreteness-abstractness, the "This I Believe" test developed by Harvey, correlated .30 with F scale scores, apparently indicating a tendency for those higher on the F scale to be more concrete than abstract in cognitive functioning. Incidentally, the correlations were high between F and dogmatism scores for extreme groups on these scales.

Harvey (1963) summarized a series of his own studies on authoritarianism. The topics of these studies ranged from attempts to influence the autokinetic movement and the effects of extreme anchors on judged weight to attitude change through role playing and the effects of exposure to descriptions of personality purportedly from friends. The results permitted some general conclusions. First, on several measures, evidence demonstrated that authoritarianism led to faster and more rigid structuring of novel material. Second, the notion that authoritarians try to ward off changes in their concepts (rigidity) was supported, but it was demonstrated that they placed heavy dependence on external cues. Apparently this paradox was resolved through distortion; for example, discrepancies were forgotten or underestimated, resulting in bland memories of anxious moments. Finally, authoritarian subjects showed less discrimination on concepts that were highly central to them. The finding of Berkowitz (1960) regarding judgment of traits in a stressful situation gave support to that interpretation.

Cognitive rigidity and haste in resolving conceptual ambiguities seem to be characteristic of authoritarian persons. Before becoming apparent, such modes of functioning, however, may require novel material, situations involving real concern, and the absence of structural constraint.

II. DOGMATISM AND ANXIETY

Previously, we gave a brief outline of the concept of dogmatism as developed by Rokeach and the characterization of dogmatism as "general" authoritarianism (as contrasted to rightwing authoritarianism). Conceptually, dogmatism is a stylistic attribute, relatively free from specific belief prescriptions. Through a structurally closed system of beliefs and disbeliefs, the highly dogmatic person defends himself against anxiety by reliance on authority and sharp, categorical rejection of beliefs not consonant with his established values. Since dogmatism represents an alternative formulation of authoritarianism and is regarded as closely related to anxiety, we will discuss the two together, digressing somewhat to give a fuller description of dogmatism.

According to Rokeach, dogmatism is discriminably different from rigidity in that the former refers to attachment to a whole system of beliefs, while rigidity represents an inflexibility of individual beliefs or behaviors. The two characteristics do not necessarily go together. Part of the series of experiments reported by Rokeach (1960) attempted to mark this distinction. With subjects selected to represent the various combinations of both high and low rigidity* and high and low dogmatism, the results yielded some evidence for the distinction; that is, it was possible to find some effects of rigidity with dogmatism held constant and vice versa. In spite of this when correlational data were used, there was a consistent positive relationship between rigidity and dogmatism (the correlations range from .37 to .55). Though rigidity is a correlate, its role in the theory of dogmatism appears to be nonessential. Because rigidity is one of several possible expressions of authoritarianism, as conceived by Adorno and others, the relationship of the two theories could use further clarification here.

A series of problem-solving experiments helped to validate the theory of dogmatism. In test sessions subjects had to deal with novel materials, to create a "cosmology" in which objects do unfamiliar things, and to work out solutions to problems in this novel "world." Subjects were selected from the extremes of distributions of scores on the dogmatism scale. Supportive evidence suggested that those scoring high on dogmatism (those with relatively "closed" minds) would perform more poorly in the problem-solving situations. Rokeach argued that the differences found lie in the "synthesis" portion of the problem-solving process, but the data underlying this conclusion were weak, because measures were rough and probably difficult to replicate. In addition the research found more rejection of unfamiliar musical compositions and greater difficulty in perceptual organization among those scoring high on dogmatism.

* The measure of rigidity was the Gough-Sanford Rigidity Scale, consisting of items indicating inflexible habits. It is interesting to note that Rokeach found a significant negative correlation between the Rigidity scores and ACE scores (1960, p. 195).

"Disbelief" systems form an integral part of the theory of dogmatism and are analogous to the rejection aspect of authoritarianism (Adorno and others). Disbeliefs are pictured as arranged along a continuum of similarity to the individual's beliefs. In an exploratory study on subjects of different religious groups those higher on dogmatism showed greater rejection of disbeliefs.

Dogmatism is viewed as a causal factor producing variation in problem-solving performance, acceptance of new forms of culture, and rejection of disbeliefs. In this type of formulation the investigator must rule out alternative explanations for his findings, and this criterion presents difficulties. Since most of the experiments reported involved selecting extreme scorers, the validity of the dogmatism scale is crucial. In the studies reported perhaps the scale actually selected those with high and low fear of failure. In fact, there was no difference between high and low dogmatics on "defection" from an unworkable system, but the comments indicated that those scoring high on the dogmatism scale were more upset and anxious. Second, if response bias is a factor, selection may determine results stemming from correlates of response set (for example, overconformity); third, in an analysis of reported childhood experiences where medium range scorers on dogmatism were included, some of the more extreme cases of glorification of parents, narrow identification, and various anxiety symptoms turned up in the middle group. This finding raises some problems in using extreme groups for study (Hyman, 1955).

Anxiety is a central concept in the theory of dogmatism with highly dogmatic people more anxious or more vulnerable to anxiety. In reporting two factor analyses (Rokeach and Fruchter, 1956; Fruchter, Rokeach, and Novak, 1958) that included scores on the dogmatism scale plus a variety of other scores, Rokeach (1960) concluded that dogmatism and anxiety are "part of a single psychological factor" (p. 349). Authoritarianism, as measured by the F scale, looked somewhat different in the analyses. However, the results of the two factor analyses were not identical, indicating that dogmatism is not equivalent to anxiety. The relationship seemed to depend on what other variables were included. For several sample groups the straight correlations between dogmatism and a measure of anxiety ranged from .36 to .64, indicating about the same covariance as that between dogmatism and rigidity. By group, it appears that high dogmatism scores were associated with high scores on anxiety scales (although the results were found principally among groups of Catholics), but the unusual and unexpected finding of a group with quite high dogmatism scores and low anxiety scores poses a problem in interpretation. This group (English communist students) was quite small (N=13) but evoked a lengthy explanation by Rokeach. He said it may be that the demands and opportunities for total dedication and activation in the communist movement "soaked up" anxiety but reinforced dogmatism. This adds an important dimension to the theory, one that has as yet received little attention.

Fillenbaum and Jackman (1961) repeated Rokeach's basic problem-solving experiment. In addition to finding that subjects scoring low on the dogmatism scale solved the problems faster than those scoring high, they also reported a moderate relationship between dogmatism scores and a measure of anxiety. The authors interpreted their results as supporting Rokeach's theory. Adams and Vidulich (1962) found that more dogmatic subjects had more difficulty learning a list of "incongruent" associates (e.g., hog-neat), and the authors interpreted this as caused by anxiety.

It might be said that, in theory, authoritarianism is a response to anxiety—a way of handling psychological tensions which threaten to overwhelm the individual. It represents a systematic and pervasive mode for handling anxieties. However, in the development and maintenance of social behavior, there are many alternatives for dealing with anxieties. From the findings presented here, we cannot yet specify the causal sequences involved in the relationship between anxiety and authoritarian responses. Because of the theoretical importance of the role of anxiety, however, it deserves more attention. The topic will be considered further when we examine some of the beliefs which have been related to authoritarianism.

III. PSYCHOPATHOLOGY

Conceptions of mental illness and maladjustment and their relationship to authoritarianism have received little attention. In the original work by Adorno and the Berkeley group the clinical portion of the investigation focused on characterizing development and expression of authoritarianism. Whether it related to mental illness or to particular pathological patterns of personality remained in the background. As Freedman, Webster, and Sanford (1956) indicated, the original work did not answer the question of the relationship of authoritarianism to psychopathology. In fact, it appeared that psychopathology might be more characteristic of those scoring in the middle range on the F scale. Studies subsequent to *The Authoritarian Personality* failed to find an association between authoritarianism and mental illness; this lack of association sometimes was interpreted as counter to expectations (see Freedman and others, 1956). The few studies we will discuss all deal with "normal" groups of respondents so that the results cannot illuminate relationships between authoritarianism and extreme forms of pathology.

PERSONALITY CHARACTERISTICS

Freedman and his colleagues suggested that the person low in authoritarianism uses impunitive means of handling hostility, may be overcontrolled, and uses repression as a defense mechanism more than a high scorer. They based their conclusions upon correlations between the F scale and clinical scales of the Minnesota Multiphasic Personality Inventory, augmented by profile comparisons based on the MMPI scales. In the two samples of freshmen women studied by the authors, the Hysteria scale, minus the somatic items, showed moderate negative relationships with scores on the F scale. Other statistically significant correlations were reported characterizing high and low authoritarians; these relationships were generally low (only 4 of 24 are over .20) and attained *statistical* significance only because of the large number of cases involved. The correlations with the Hysteria scale were probably not due to response bias, however, because Couch and Keniston found essentially no association in their sample between this scale and the tendency to agree with statements on a wide variety of content.

Siegel (1956) obtained results that at the outset appear self-contradictory. On a set of questions designed to measure manifest hostility, persons scoring higher on the F scale appear more hostile than those obtaining lower F scale scores. This finding held for both a college student group and for a patient group at a veteran's clinic. On a projective test of hostility derived from Rorschach responses, non-authoritarians among the patients appeared more hostile than authoritarians. Students tested did not show this association. Siegel concluded tentatively that those low in authoritarianism tended to express their hostility in ways different from the more authoritarian individuals.

Attempts to study aggressive reactions face several problems. At the theoretical level, there is the problem of what reactions to expect from authoritarian persons—more overt aggression by reason of generalized hostility or less by reason of submissiveness and conventionality; does the authoritarian individual simmer more at deeper levels or are his impulses displaced or projected? Whatever the theoretical stance, measuring such variables is difficult, especially by paper-and-pencil tests, in which the level of response obtained is questionable. For example, Plant, Telford, and Thomas (1965), using a battery of psychological tests, found a group of freshman students scoring high on dogmatism to be impulsive, defensive, conventional, and stereotyped in thinking. Yet Abrams (1965) found no significant relationship between authoritarianism (as measured by F scale scores) and overt aggressive actions in a "war" game. (The game was designed to provide opportunity for aggression at little cost to the player.)

Kogan (1956) studied the relationship between repression and authoritarianism, noting that the methods Adorno and associates used to show this relationship have been since seriously questioned. Assuming that repression would produce relative inability to hear sexual and aggressive sentences masked with noise, Kogan studied college students' ability to identify correctly such sentences. Using neutral passages as a control, he found that high scorers on the F scale reported hearing fewer of the sexual and aggressive sentences. With intelligence (as measured by a verbal test) held constant, the associations remained at the same level. Another study, however, found an inverse relationship between authoritarianism and preference for repressive defense mechanisms. Using a test of repression-sensitization, Byrne, Blaylock, and Goldberg (1966) found that F scale scores were associated positively with sensitization. The results suggested that alternative mechanisms of defense, including intellectualization, reflect the social milieu while still serving to ward off the emotional consequences of anxiety-arousing material.

In his discussion of authoritarian attitudes and psychopathology, Jensen (1957) considered several different measures of authoritarianism. Employing the prejudice (Pr) scale developed by Gough from the MMPI as a personality measure of authoritarianism, Jensen reported the relationship between Pr and the MMPI clinical scales, concluding that maladjustment was indeed associated with authoritarianism in students studied. However, the pattern of associations was subject to response bias in the light of Couch and Keniston's (1960) analysis of yeasaying tendencies measured by the scales of the MMPI (cp. Rorer, 1965; Peabody, 1966). Contamination also was possible because both predictor and criterion were derived from the same measuring device. The correlation between Pr and F (r=.27) is suspect as Pr correlated .51 with a measure of acquiescence set. Jensen's study added the interesting finding, however, that scores of students judged by faculty members to be maladjusted were significantly higher than scores of students considered to be adjusted. Although many values may have influenced these faculty judgments, it is unlikely that agreeing tendencies in the students could have accounted for the high relationship found.

This necessarily brief venture into psychopathology leaves most questions unanswered. On neither absolute nor relative grounds can authoritarian persons be characterized empirically as more (or less) pathological. Many, if not all, of the more popular criteria of mental health are normative and vary among groups. Authoritarian characteristics could be positive factors in "adjustment" in certain situations or cultures. However, within the broad set of norms with which we are most familiar the conception of authoritarianism maintains that the underlying problems contributing to authoritarianism and the devices or directions taken to solve these problems are very costly in a psychological sense. Refinement in detailing these costs both conceptually and at the measurement level is needed. Generally, the student of authoritarianism thinks of it as maladjustive, but more rigorous research (and sampling) is required to verify this assumption.

Authoritarianism
and Related Beliefs

A great many studies of authoritarianism deal with the relationships between authoritarian personality traits and beliefs. Some of the beliefs investigated have been specific and some general. We have categorized them, based on content, into political beliefs (including participation in and conception of political processes, plus views of nations and international relations); religious beliefs; attitudes toward family and childrearing; alienation; social perception; and ethnic beliefs.

Most studies reviewed in this section conceptualized authoritarianism as a relatively fixed characteristic of personality. Authoritarianism was often treated as causally antecedent to the beliefs studied: authoritarianism is an independent variable which disposes an individual toward acceptance of certain beliefs. Sometimes, however, alternatives to F scale authoritarianism, as an explanatory concept, were offered. While most alternatives offered were "response bias" interpretations (i.e., a relationship between F scale scores and another variable is held to be spurious or uninterpretable), other alternative explanations dealt with content. In the latter type of study, F scale authoritarianism was viewed as a special case (for example, of dogmatism). Finally, some studies examined relationships between authoritarianism and a set of beliefs very similar to authoritarianism, though frequently called by some other name.

The search for beliefs concomitant with authoritarianism presents a logical difficulty in using the F scale as a measure of personality functioning, since the F scale itself measures beliefs. The items of the F scale, for the most part, assess beliefs about people (e.g., "Most of our social problems would be solved if we could somehow get rid of the immoral, crooked, and feeble-minded people"; "Nowadays more and more people are prying into matters that should remain personal and private").* Correlates of the F scale, then, show relationships among beliefs. While this difficulty may be due to methodological shortcomings of the questionnaire approach that may be ameliorated by including a wide variety of content, it is at least in part a conceptual problem. Beliefs about the character, conduct, and interpersonal relations of people are at the core of the theory of authoritarianism. While authoritarianism at one level constitutes a grouping of general beliefs, studies relating authoritarianism to political, religious, or other beliefs supply more specific content. Most of the studies reviewed attempted to do this. The beliefs measured by the F scale *may* be viewed, however, as attitudinal rather than as solely expressive or stylistic (e.g., Siegel and Siegel, 1957).

The search for correlates of a major variable is quite a common pattern in social psychology. The initial work may specify that authoritarianism includes characteristics *a, b,* and *c,* for example. Subsequent investigations expand the list to include *d, e,* and *f.* In this way, many specific items

* A number of the items in the dogmatism scale are also of this type.

of psychological content are subsumed under a more general heading. Whatever defects characterize the workmanship on the original conceptualization and data, however, carry over to the subsequent extensions.

I. POLITICAL BELIEFS AND BEHAVIOR

In *The Authoritarian Personality* concern with potentially antidemocratic aspects of personality played an important role, with the highly authoritarian person drawn as submissive to powerful figures, discomforted by the ambiguity and uncertainties of democratic processes, and rejecting toward different or unfamiliar groups. The book implied an ultimate concern with the political outlook and behavior of authoritarians. Because of the negative implications of authoritarianism for democratic political systems, it is not surprising that later investigators sought to specify types of political beliefs suggested by authoritarianism.

Authoritarianism of the political right and left has been discussed by Shils (in Christie and Jahoda, 1954), who concluded that the F scale studies dealt with rightwing manifestations only. In this connection, Rokeach's work on dogmatism set out explicitly to develop an instrument to measure authoritarianism of all political persuasions. His treatment represented an alternative explanation of the causal sequence connecting beliefs and personality which included F scale authoritarianism as a special case. In the *Open and Closed Mind,* however, Rokeach maintained that bigotry (including political intolerance) is associated more with the right than with the left. Although he found leftist groups who were relatively dogmatic and opinionated (but low on the F and antisemitism scales), Rokeach argued from his overall results that the closed-minded individual, at least in modern political systems, is more likely to subscribe to conservative ideology. Studies by Barker (1963), however, indicated that bigotry is not exclusive to rightest ideologies.

In the United States allegiance to a particular political party does not seem to be related to authoritarianism (see McClosky, 1958; Campbell, Converse, Miller, and Stokes, 1960). Yet political and economic conservatism is often reported as positively associated with F scale scores (for example, Levinson, 1957). The scale most frequently employed (the PEC scale of conservatism) suffers from potential response bias, so this may account for much of the relationship found. In addition, the distinction between conservatism in the economic realm and conservatism in other areas must be emphasized (Lipset, 1960), because putting them together may obscure relationships to other variables. Party allegiance as a variable includes a great many elements. Perhaps it is not surprising that such a crude classification does not relate to authoritarianism, especially considering the diversity of interests included in our political parties.

Two studies by Leventhal, Jacobs and Kudirka (1964) attempted to assess the role of ideology in voters' choice of candidates for office. Using a short but balanced form of the F scale, researchers found that a group of Yale students with high scores preferred Nixon and the Republican party to Kennedy and the Democratic party. The authors regarded that particular choice as indicative of the high salience of conservative vs. liberal values. A followup study presented pairs of hypothetical candidates to a group of subjects, the choices including all possible combinations of liberal-conservative and Republican-Democrat. When candidate ideology was not considered, there was no relationship of F scale scores to choice; when party was disregarded, however, the authoritarian subjects preferred the conservative candidate.

Participation in political activities seems to be related inversely to authoritarianism (Janowitz and Marvick, 1953). But, Lane (1955) reported some relationships between authoritarianism and electoral choice which do not fit a simple interpretation. He found no difference in frequency of voting between authoritarian and nonauthoritarian persons. Education was controlled in this analysis, and a four-item Guttman scale composed of modified F and E scale statements measured authoritarianism. When considered separately level of education related negatively to scores on authoritarianism. Lane found possible differences in the motivation to vote. The nonauthoritarian respondents had a greater sense of political efficacy, while the authoritarians reported membership in more groups, which Lane argued led to more social pressure to conform. One of the most interesting findings was that among the Republicans those low on the authoritarianism measure thought government was not doing enough in welfare, unemployment, and related areas, while those high on authoritarianism thought government did too much. There was no difference among the Democrats where both high and low authoritarian groups thought government was not doing enough. A study of ward chairmen in New Haven (Harned, 1961) revealed that those leaders high on a measure of authoritarianism put more emphasis on party organization but were *less* ideologically partisan than those low on authoritarianism.

Paralleling authoritarianism research was the development of a general measure of conservatism by McClosky (1958). His measure consisted of a series of items expressing conservative ideology (e.g., about ownership of private property), but not specifically political in nature. Using a sample of 1,200 adults in Minneapolis, McClosky administered a questionnaire with several different scales to measure personality variables. He found little relationship between the measure of conservatism and party affiliation, economic attitudes, or the political designation which the respondent applied to himself. A person who called himself a political conservative was not necessarily a conservative as measured by the scale. Scores on the conservatism scale itself were negatively related to education. The extreme conservatives were higher on measures of dominance, anomie, alienation, pessimism, and guilt and lower on self-confidence and social responsibility. In addition, the conservative was characterized as more hostile, contemptuous of weakness, rigid, paranoid, and intolerant of human frailty. The study claimed the relationships recorded held with educational and status levels controlled, so the results were not due primarily to differences in education or sophistication.

Given the relationships found by McClosky, conservatism appeared to resemble authoritarianism and is included here as a parallel to it in conception. A further similarity—and a disturbing one—appeared in McClosky's remark that the conservative tended to agree with broad, obscure items; acquiescence may be a problem in McClosky's findings.

Studies of political attitudes by Campbell, Converse, Miller, and Stokes (1960) used McClosky's conservatism scale. Selection of respondents was by nationwide probability sampling. As in previous works, the measure of conservatism related negatively to educational level and social status; also, the degree of conservatism increased with age. There was little relationship, however, between conservatism scores and opinions about specific issues of social welfare and international relations. Again, conservatism and political party preference did not relate.

In further analyses, Campbell, Converse, Miller, and Stokes found that for those who had changed their party identification for some reason other than a social one, there was a clear relationship between the party chosen and the conservatism score. Those who moved from Democrat to Republican identification had higher scores than those moving in the opposite direction. The authors explained this as a reflection of the greater degree of ideological organization and consistency characteristic of those who consciously changed their political affiliation. Hence, the link between party preference and conservatism held true only under certain conditions.

Previously, we noted Lipset's conclusion that authoritarianism is more characteristic of the lower classes. He used survey evidence from a variety of sources showing that the poorer strata are more intolerant. The social situation of the poor with little education, little participation in organizations, economic insecurity, and relatively isolated occupations, forestalls a sophisticated view of the political structure, making members of this class vulnerable to extremist appeals. In this connection, Lipset made a crucial point about social structure: commitments to democratic values, institutions, and procedures (for example, membership in a trade union) can override predispositions toward authoritarianism. The expression of authoritarian attitudes may be modified by social attachments which conflict or compete with these predispositions.

In political surveys reviewed in Campbell, Converse, Miller, and Stokes, two short versions of the F scale (one with reversed items) were used. General authoritarianism did not relate to beliefs about specific political issues; in fact, the scores showed little relationship to any other variable. The only positive finding was that college educated respondents with high scores displayed more hostility toward minority groups. As a result of their experience with the items, these investigators dropped F scale type measures.

Libo (1957) reported no relationship between scores on the F scale and a measure of attitudes toward socialized medicine for a group of 97 senior medical students. As a group, the respondents scored low on the F scale and rejected socialized medicine. Libo commented that a relationship between a personality characteristic and a social attitude is more likely to be found where the attitude is *not* a salient part of the group's ideology. Otherwise, there are constraints on the expression of a personal value system. These comments are important in determining causes of authoritarian attitudes and the role of authoritarianism as a causal variable.

Relationships between political beliefs and authoritarianism seem to require further conceptualization at this point. Few specific beliefs show clear relationships to authoritarian dispositions, and methodological refinements must precede investigation of some promising leads (for example, elaboration of potential hypotheses in Lipset's book). According to Rokeach's approach, people who were generally authoritarian could hold any specific belief, because the crucial thing is the manner in which the beliefs are held. If, as indicated in Campbell, Converse, Miller, and Stokes, most people's beliefs are neither very consistent nor very ideological, then a different approach to the relevance of authoritarianism for political beliefs must be employed. There are, unquestionably, specific groups for whom ideology is important—for example, the students studied by Leventhal and associates (1964)—yet an individual may be authoritarian and have no interest in political affairs. Evidence indicates that where events can be interpreted in various ways and the social constraints are not potent, authoritarian persons will construe things in line with their personality dispositions (McCarthy and Johnson, 1962; and Williams, 1963).

Hofstadter (1965) discussed recurrent episodes of radical right sentiment. Such diverse political movements as anti-Catholicism and free silver in the nineteenth century and

McCarthyism and Goldwater conservatism in the twentieth reflected a similar central "paranoid style," he said. Although describing participants as closed-minded in their espousal of causes, Hofstadter's primary interest lay in political events rather than personality. At the level of the social movement, Hofstadter maintained, the origins of the paranoid style reside in conflict and alienation, a clash of irreconcilable interests.

Originally, Hofstadter attributed the basis for the movements discussed to projective rationalizations growing out of social stress. The occurence of these political outbreaks requires a strong sense of nationalism, political channels, and sufficient social disorder to arouse widespread identity crises. He cited Goldwater's 1964 campaign as an example.

A later discussion of the paranoid style gave more emphasis to the role of economic conservatism and the channeling of fundamentalist orientation into vocal protest. Hofstadter maintained these factors contribute to the growth of a movement, resulting in a group that seeks redress for wrongs they attribute to a vast conspiracy (for example, the alleged threat of an internal communist conspiracy). However, the ideology of leaders and the forces creating a radical group cannot be attributed automatically to the group's followers. Nor are the forces which set in motion a movement necessarily the same ones that maintain it.

Presumably, authoritarianism would predispose an individual toward sympathy with, and perhaps participation in, the kind of political manifestation which Hofstadter terms "paranoid." Certainly, the externalization of blame and the uncompromising moral tone of these rightist movements resemble authoritarian style. Hofstadter regarded the individual who manifests the paranoid style as closed-minded in Rokeach's sense. As an example, he cited those believing that fluoridation is used to derange the faculties of loyal

Americans in preparation for communist takeover. But can modes of cognitive functioning be inferred from involvement in a particular issue or movement? Evidence suggests a common core of people join a number of protest groups, including organizations fighting fluoridation, communism, mental health, "artificial" food, and the United Nations. Even at the belief level, however, much more evidence concerning the distribution and generality of closed-mindedness is needed before specific conclusions can be drawn.

How does the authoritarian person function in a political system and how does his behavior affect political institutions? Greenstein (1965) raised these questions in a valuable review of authoritarianism and political processes. Connections between personality and *specific* political beliefs are still problematic, he noted. There was a "tendency in the original reports [*The Authoritarian Personality*] to discuss the ethnically prejudiced and politically conservative attitudes of many authoritarians as if these were part of the defining characteristics of the syndrome itself" (p. 92). Greenstein concluded that authoritarianism did not necessarily lead either to fascist beliefs or to particular political activity. We cannot predict forward from personality to political behavior. Nor, apparently, can authoritarianism be attributed to those involved in particular activities because, as Greenstein observed, social movements and institutions are born and maintained by numerous forces. Both the crucial characteristics of those who are active in social movements, on one hand, and the political activities of authoritarian persons, on the other, are problems requiring clarification through more research effort. The relationship of the "paranoid" style in political life and the authoritarian personality warrants investigation.

Investigators have studied links between beliefs about international affairs and authoritarianism. A major part of the concept of authoritarianism is made up of ethnocentric attitudes. In a general way, ethnocentrism subsumes reactions to things patriotic and foreign, as well as race prejudice (the latter aspect of ethnocentric attitudes is discussed below). In addition, one social science approach to problems of international relations involves study of attitudes and beliefs.

Levinson (1957) decribed nationalism as a "facet of a broad ethnocentric orientation" expressed as beliefs which are either "isolationist" or "imperialistic." In either form, the distinction between the ingroup and the outgroup is crucial in defining ethnocentrism. To explore this conception, Levinson developed a scale for measuring nationalist orientation. (For example, one item read: "The immigration of foreigners to this country should be cut down so that we can provide for Americans first.") The form of the scale is familiar, resembling the F scale. In fact, the scores on the nationalism scale showed a moderate positive correlation with F scale scores. They also related positively to measures of ethnocentrism, political and economic conservatism (PEC scale), traditional family ideology, and religious conventionalism. All of these measuring instruments suffer to some degree from format problems.

The general hypothesis in these investigations is that the individual's thinking about the social organization in which he lives will reflect his personality structure. Levinson cautioned that the degree of ideological reflection of personality varies among persons and varies with the social setting. These important qualifications often have been ignored.

Various studies have linked authoritarianism and attitudes on international relations. Smith and Rosen (1958) developed a measure of "world-mindedness," including items such as: "All national governments ought to be abolished and replaced by one central world government." Items were worded in both "agree" and "disagree" directions to control for response bias. Respondents scoring high and low on this scale differed significantly in their F scale scores with the more world-minded scoring lower on the F scale. More important, Smith and Rosen conducted intensive interviews on topics relevant to the scales with 40 respondents scoring in the extremes. The interview material was coded without knowledge of the respondent's answers on the scales. The interview responses showed the more world-minded individuals as more equalitarian in their outlook and less apt to hold stereotypes. These individuals also viewed the causes of various personal problems as internal rather than external, showed optimism about the possibility that society's problems would be solved, and chose as ideal persons those known for humanistic, intellectual, and humanitarian endeavors (the difference between Albert Schweitzer and General MacArthur, for whatever it's worth). Subjects were a small sample of summer school students, raising the frequently encountered difficulties of generalizing from the sample to larger groups.

On a more concrete topic, MacKinnon and Centers (1956b) surveyed attitudes toward relations between the United States and Russia. The schedule included questions about whether the United States should trade with Russia in nonstrategic goods and whether students in this country should be taught about the USSR. Respondents were an approximate cross section of Los Angeles residents. By means of scores based on F. Sanford's short version of the F scale (F. Sanford, 1950), the whole sample was divided into "equalitarians" and "authoritarians." For the most part, the responses favored both trade and education, but the equalitarian respondents were much more positive in their approval. Examining the reasons given by respondents to support their positions, MacKinnon and Centers found international benefits and good relations mentioned more often by the equalitarian respondents. Authoritarians mentioned punitiveness more often as a reason against trade and economic benefit as a reason in favor of trade. The investigators concluded that different propaganda appeals might work better for those high and those low on authoritarianism.

In a later report, these same authors (MacKinnon and Centers, 1963) noted that authoritarian respondents less frequently than the nonauthoritarians considered themselves informed about the Russian system, yet they were more convinced of the correctness of their opinions. The latter finding was interpreted as reflecting greater exposure to diverse groups for those *low* on authoritarianism.

The theoretical relevance of the study is limited by the lack of control over the respondents' educational level. Many of the reasons reportedly given by equalitarian respondents clearly came from well-educated persons.

Gladstone and Taylor (1958) found general attitudes of belligerence, nonpacification, and feelings of threat regarding international events to be interrelated. As in works on authoritarianism, the authors interpreted the hostile attitudes of their subjects as projections of unacceptable impulses. In similar fashion, Rosenberg (1958) developed a scale measuring "faith in people" (one item: "If you don't watch yourself, people will take advantage of you"). Subjects scoring high on this scale tended to reject the idea of power in international relations, to see the United Nations as a more effective deterrent to war than nuclear weapons, and to emphasize understanding of others over military power.

Christiansen (1959) explored some links between personality and attitudes toward foreign relations. Although not directly concerned with authoritarianism, Christiansen examined a series of theoretical positions which hypothesize relationships between personality functioning and beliefs about foreign affairs, including generalization of everyday reactions, frustration-aggression, displacement of inner conflicts, and others. Preferences for reactions to a set of international situations constituted the basic measure. These preferences were classified according to form (threat oriented *vs.* problem oriented) and direction (external, internal, passive). The study took place in Norway, using applicants to the Military and Naval Academy as subjects.

Through imaginative and thorough use of several measuring devices, the investigator obtained information regarding preferences for reactions to everyday frustrations, psychological conflicts (scored from responses to modified Blacky pictures), manifest insecurity, and nationalism. The results showed a consistency between the style of everyday reactions and international reactions; there were positive relationships between the number of inner conflicts exhibited by subjects and preferences for aggressive international reactions, and between patriotism and an aggressive international stance. Although the findings proved complex and not entirely in line with expectations, they indicated that nationalist sentiment mediates the degree to which displaced aggression fastens onto foreign affairs. In addition, the generalization of everyday reaction tendencies to international settings appeared to be mediated by nationalism. An overall index of destructive international attitudes showed positive associations with nationalism, psychodynamic conflicts, and aggression in everyday situations.

These findings are important for understanding the way in which authoritarian personality functioning can influence beliefs about international affairs. The impact of personality on those beliefs progresses through intermediate steps in which the beliefs serve instrumental functions for the person. One potential linkage is through learned responses to conflict situations. Normative constraints would play a significant role here. The other involves the centrality of nationalist beliefs in the individual's ideological structure. Social norms would be an important factor in the learning and maintenance of nationalism. The tie between self-conception and nationalist sentiment and symbols appears to be a crucial variable in responses to international issues.

At present the relation between political beliefs and authoritarianism is not clear. Authoritarianism of the right seems related to aspects of nationalism and anti-world-mindedness. Specific aspects of international relations may or may not be related. Beliefs similar to components of authoritarianism, such as misanthropy, seem associated with a hostile approach to international relations. There are difficulties. First, doubts about the relation of education to some of the findings raises the suspicion that many reported responses represent only superficial beliefs. Second, the relationships in studies of political beliefs between conservatism or authoritarianism and specific issues of social welfare and foreign affairs are not consistent. There appears to be growing recognition of the contribution of social and cognitive factors that mediate the expression of personality in beliefs and behavior.

II. RELIGIOUS BELIEFS

Generally, the relationship of authoritarianism to religion is theoretically similar to its relationship to political beliefs; given certain personality dispositions, certain religious content usually is more congenial. Because of the organized structure of religion and its place in systems of childrearing and training, some imply, however, that authoritarianism is partly a consequence of religious orientation. Investigators sometimes view religious systems as fostering authoritarian persons. For example, investigators not uncommonly treat Catholics as a "known" group of relatively authoritarian personalities.

Rokeach found that a group of Catholic students scored relatively high on the dogmatism and opinionation scales, as well as on the F and ethnocentrism scales. Catholic samples had higher F scale scores in a study reported by Warshay, Goldman, and Biddle (1964). Gregory (1957) reported a positive relationship between a test of "orthodox religious beliefs" and F scale scores. His subjects included several groups of fundamentalists, but, unfortunately, Gregory's "sample" was an unsystematic hodgepodge of sects and students. The religious groups were small and were composed of older persons with relatively little education. Also, it is not clear (and this is a general criticism) whether the respondents perceived the relevance of their religion to the testing. Arousing a set to respond as a "Catholic," "Jew," "Boy Scout," or whatever yields more orthodox answers where the group serves a positive reference function (see, for example, Hovland, Janis, and Kelley, 1953).

Lipset theorized that the factors predisposing low status people toward authoritarianism were the same ones responsible for the appeal of fundamentalist religious beliefs. In addition, he cited studies indicating that in Holland and Sweden communism found more strength in regions that were once centers of fundamentalism and that where communism is a *major* party, its chief support comes from lower income groups.

Some religious beliefs fit more easily into authoritarian patterns, and the cognitive structure of authoritarianism finds particular types of religion more congenial. Bible-belt fundamentalism can be quite authoritarian (Shils, in Christie and Jahoda, 1954), yet not all authoritarian persons belong to fundamentalist sects, nor do fundamentalists necessarily

display authoritarianism. Extremist, authoritarian movements exhibit many different forms and contents (Hoffer,
1958).

The relation of authoritarianism to major religious groups
presents complex problems for interpretation. Photiadis
and Johnson (1963) obtained data on church participation,
orthodox beliefs, prejudice, and certain personality variables,
including authoritarianism, from a sample of 300 Protestant
church members in a South Dakota town. Even with other
variables controlled, orthodoxy was positively related to
authoritarianism, leading to the interpretation that authoritarianism was the link between orthodoxy and prejudice.
Since orthodoxy was also associated with church participation, which in turn was not related to authoritarianism and
negatively related to prejudice, the authors concluded that
greater participation produced greater tolerance. Religion
thus played a dual role in group relationships.

Cross-cultural studies shed some further light on the
relationship of religion and authoritarianism. Weima (1965)
found for both Catholic and Protestant groups in the
Netherlands a positive relationship between F scale scores
and religious conservatism. Rejection of other religious
groups varied positively with authoritarianism. These findings supported those of Photiadis and Johnson. Authoritarian outlook may affect orthodoxy within a religious group
and lead to rejection of other religions. In Western culture
a strong historical tie between orthodox belief and hostility
toward other faiths exists. Such relationships undoubtedly
reflect, to some degree, the social pressures arising within
these institutions. The dominant groups in an organized
religion can create pressures toward conservatism and sharp-
en contrasts with nonbelievers.

At the group level, however, authoritarianism and ethnocentrism are not always related. In an Australian study,

Knopfelmacher and Armstrong (1963), using modified versions of the F and E scales, tested high school students of various religions (including Catholics, Jews, and several Protestant groups). As expected, Catholics scored highest on the F scale, but lowest on a measure of social distance. E scale scores showed no relationship to religious group. That Catholics appeared as more authoritarian *and* more accepting of others than the other respondents was unusual. It may have reflected the influence of a cultural setting on the functioning of a religious institution.

III. AUTHORITARIANISM AND THE FAMILY

According to the theory underlying the authoritarian personality, authoritarians are made and not born. Therefore, the family appears to provide an important research area in studying the authoritarian personality. In this section we consider studies of authoritarianism and attitudes about childrearing and studies of authoritarianism in children as related to family patterns.

Levinson and Huffman (1955) developed a measure of autocratic family ideology, the Traditional Family Ideology (TFI) scale. The items, taken largely from clinical interviews, covered five areas: conventionalism, authoritarian submission, exaggerated masculinity and femininity, extreme emphasis on discipline, and moralistic rejection of impulse life. On the basis of data gathered from 42 female and 67 male night school college students, the authors reported a correlation of .73 with a 10-item version of the original F scale. The meaning of this correlation is not clear, because in 34 of 40 of the TFI items agreement indicated autocratic beliefs. This, coupled with the fact of identical scoring for F scale items, raises serious questions of acquiescence. The authors presented a short form of the TFI along with "validation" data, but all of the items on the short form suffered from the same potential response bias.

Positive, but low, relationships between F scale scores and authoritarian childrearing attitudes in college students were found by Kates and Diab (1955). Using the Parent Attitude Survey (Shoben, 1949) as a measure of childrearing attitudes, the authors reported positive correlations, based on data from the female subjects, of .28 to .34 between F scale scores and "desire to keep the child subordinate and conforming" and "emphasis on keeping the child dependent." No such relationships for the males were found. The third dimension measured by the instrument, disregard of the child as an individual, related positively to authoritarianism for the males ($r=.29$), but not for the females ($r=.02$). With the Parent Attitude Survey validated on mothers of problem children vs. mothers of nonproblem children, the authors concluded that authoritarian female students often have attitudes regarding childrearing similar to mothers of problem children. The measure of childrearing attitudes is largely free from acquiescence bias.

Breaking away from the limitation of student subjects, Hart (1957) interviewed mothers of preschool children, covering six areas of parent-child interaction: independence, dependence, cleanliness-toilet training, feeding, sex, and aggression. Responses were classified as exhibiting love, nonlove, and ambiguity. He found, first, that the nonlove oriented treatment correlated highly with F scale scores ($r=.63$), second, that in areas of sex and aggression, authoritarian mothers did not show more nonlove responses than in other areas. The interviews also indicated that the nonauthoritarian mother attempted to maintain the child's approach tendency toward her, as measured by ratings of the interview material.

A study by Adams, Schwab, and Aponte (1965) compared

73

parents of 17 children between the ages of 5 and 15 who had been referred to a medical center for psychiatric evaluation with the parents of 17 control children matched according to age, sex, ordinal position, and intelligence. Expecting that "fascist-conservative" parents would generate maladjustment in their children, the authors administered the F scale, the TFI, E, and PEC scales. Only the PEC scale, measuring conservatism, yielded significant differences between control and experimental groups, and the *control* group parents were higher. The authors concluded this greater conservatism may have resulted from the fact that, inadvertently, the control parents in the sample enjoyed somewhat higher incomes than the experimental group. Other data in this study derived from interviews with parents measured the extent to which parents could take the role of the child (i.e., consider things from his perspective). The lack of such ability was considered an aspect of authoritarianism. Control parents were much more able to take the child's point of view than were the parents of referred children. The inference of antecedent authoritarianism in interpretation of this finding as reflected by the role-perspective data could be a gross error. Under the circumstances, parents discussing a child who has been referred for psychiatric evaluation and treatment, are confronted with quite a different task than those whose children simply are participating in an experiment as the control parents probably thought, although the investigators do not mention what the parents were told. Neither do they report the source of the control families.

Another approach to the study of authoritarianism in the family setting involves inferring characteristics of the home situation based on responses from children with differing authoritarianism scores. Lyle and Levitt (1955) administered an antidemocratic scale for children (CADS) to two groups of fifth grade students. Since all 24 items on this scale were worded in an F positive direction, response bias was possible. The investigators correlated scores on the CADS with responses to incomplete sentences, designed to measure parental punitiveness, and with aggression in the children (as measured by paper-and-pencil tests). In these studies the authors found that parental punitiveness correlated with both authoritarianism and aggression. For the larger group, containing 157 children, intelligence scores showed a slight inverse relationship to aggression scores (a correlation of minus .29); a negative relationship to authoritarianism (a correlation of minus .44); and no significant correlation with parental punitiveness. Even when intelligence was used for a control, the relationship between antidemocratic tendencies and parental punitiveness remained ($r=.32$ vs. $r=.33$ with IQ constant). However, controlling for intelligence reduced the correlation between antidemocratic tendencies and willingness to be aggressive from $r=.28$ to $r=.18$.

Citing studies ranging over a wider area, Frenkel-Brunswik (1954) discussed relationships of child and adult authoritarianism. Using questionnaires and interviews with children, she explored such conceptions as the good father, the good mother, good girl, teacher. She reported a parallel between the syndrome of authoritarianism in adults and in children, in that children who are prejudiced "tend to display authoritarian aggression, rigidity, cruelty, superstition, externalization and projectivity, denial of weakness, power orientation and more often hold dichotomous conceptions of sex roles, of kinds of people, and of values" (p. 237). She ascribed these differences to characteristics of the parents and the home atmosphere.

Frenkel-Brunswik noted one significant reversal between children and adults in the authoritarian syndrome. The unprejudiced child, she found, more often showed greater conformity to adults, but the author noted, "this conformity to adult values is based on genuine love and identification with the parents and is to be differentiated from the fearful submission of the ethnocentric child" (p. 243) who is inconsistently submissive. While she apparently based this conclusion upon clinical impression, she cites numerous other studies as supportive.

Richert (1963) obtained negative results in an attempt to assess antecedent conditions to authoritarianism through use of retrospective accounts by freshman psychology students. Birth order as an antecedent to authoritarianism failed to show significant relationships to F scale scores (Greenberg and others, 1963).

Two other studies explored intergenerational authoritarianism between college student respondents and their parents. Williams and Williams (1963) found that college respondents had significantly lower F scale scores than their parents (who were mailed questionnaires; return rate 44 percent). The scores of males correlated significantly (but low) with their mothers' scores (r=.28) but not with their fathers' scores (r=.12), while females' scores correlated significantly with their fathers' scores (r=.24) but not with their mothers' scores (r=.19). These cross-sex, parent-child correlations proved contrary to expectations. Byrne (1965) studied relationships between college students and parents on the F scale and the TFI (Levinson and Huffman, 1955). With all correlations below .38, he found a pattern of correlations differing from those reported by Williams and Williams. F scale scores of sons correlated significantly with those of fathers and mothers and also with the fathers' TFI scores, but not the mothers'. TFI scores of sons correlated significantly with fathers' F and TFI, but they related to neither score for mothers. The only significant correlation found for daughters was between F of the daughter and F of the mother. For these two similar studies the only point of replication was the correlation between sons and mothers on the F scale; otherwise the data failed in almost uncanny fashion to support each other.

In a study by Johnson, Johnson, and Martin (1961) college students rated a number of behaviors for sex appropriateness, one of the important aspects of authoritarianism. Those with higher F scale scores rated fewer behaviors appropriate to both sexes. Neither F scale scores nor ratings of sex roles related to occupational level; however, classifying respondents on the basis of "entrepreneurial" (self-employed or deriving income primarily from profits or fees) vs. "bureaucratic" (employed by someone else or in an organization with three or more levels) occupations of parents showed significantly higher F scale scores for the children of entrepreneurial parents. This study treated authoritarianism as antecedent to definitions of sex roles.

As is the case with other areas we have explored, results of studies of family and childrearing are fragmentary. Some important differences related to authoritarianism seem to exist, both with respect to correlates of authoritarianism and development of children's beliefs. On the other hand, the existence of class and ethnic differences in childrearing and attitudes toward the parental role are neglected factors. It would be worthwhile to consider different groups and their effects on relationships of the type reported in this section. Too often, differences in beliefs have been treated simply as individual differences, unrelated to the social structure in which they occurred.

The relevance of parental beliefs concerning authoritarianism and its correlates to an ultimate expression in a child's personality is neither immediate nor specific. Presumably, the line of influence begins with the personality and belief systems of adults, which determine their behaviors as parents; these behaviors in turn form the situation for the child, leading to patterns of response by him. None of the studies has demonstrated any direct connection between the ends of this line. Lipset's analysis of working class authoritarianism (1960) as a developmental account depends ultimately on class differences in childrearing and rather tenuous empirical support for the effects of such differences on the child's personality. The few studies outlined above suggest the need for more research in this area.

IV. ALIENATION

Alienation is a popular area in current sociology that has developed as a separate field of study in much the same way authoritarianism has. A multifaceted concept, alienation includes such notions as powerlessness, meaninglessness, normlessness, isolation, and self-estrangement. (Seeman, 1959, describes these aspects in detail.) Although the concept is formulated in a negative way (suggesting the lack of certain qualities), alienation encompasses a certain set of beliefs or values signifying feelings of isolation from the social system. Malfunctions or breakdowns in social arrangements presumably drive persons toward these alienated beliefs.

In a preceding section we noted that in several studies alienation showed positive relationships to authoritarianism (Roberts and Rokeach, 1956; Srole, 1956; Dean, 1961; McDill, 1961; Rhodes, 1961). Most commonly, the measure of alienation consisted of questionnaire items. For example, Dean (1961) developed a 24-item scale with three subparts measuring feelings of powerlessness, normlessness, and isolation. Dean's article traced briefly the history of these ideas in sociology and outlined some of the many possible correlates.

His scale contained statements such as "We are just so many cogs in the machinery of life" and "The end often justifies the means." These items show similarities to beliefs which have been included under the concept of authoritarianism.

The relationship between this measure of alienation and F scale scores, while positive, was low (Dean, 1961). An examination of the measure, as well as Srole's scale of alienation (Srole, 1956), revealed the familiar problem of response bias. The patterns of correlations reported by Dean among his subscales and between subscales and other variables, such as age, suggest that acquiescence may have accounted for some of the findings. Improved measures of alienation are essential to further research.

Davids (1955) conceptualized alienation as a set of related personality dispositions, including egocentricity, distrust, pessimism, anxiety, and resentment; his conclusion was that "People who are high on any one of these tend to be high on all of them" (Davids, p. 61). The difference between this approach to alienation and that described above is roughly the difference between a psychological and sociological approach. Davids used an ingenious variety of projective materials, recall of spoken passages, sentence completion, and clinical interviews to measure the different aspects of his alienation syndrome. The positive relationships among different aspects of alienation seem to be free from response set. Apparently, further research on the concept or its relationship to other types of alienation has not been done.

The role of authoritarianism as an explanatory concept appears to be somewhat different from the role of alienation; thus far, the two seem related simply as correlates. In their manifestations, the two concepts show some similarities (which may explain why investigators sought to relate them). Pessimism, anxiety, and distrust characterize both concepts.

However, in tracing back to the antecedents of alienation, the explanatory scheme soon diverges from the theoretical history of authoritarianism. As a dependent variable, alienation results from a series of social processes. Taken at the group level, for example, alienation represents the breakdown of a group's normative structure which leaves the members wandering in an aimless fashion. Or it may result from separation of workers from control over their work and their consequent helplessness in the face of social and economic demands. On the other hand, authoritarianism is generally conceived of as the outcome of intrapsychic conflict arising ultimately from defects in socialization. One can see both differences in the way the two concepts are developed and also some tantalizing similarities, such as the role of parental limitations in leading to both alienation and authoritarianism in their offspring. Some conditions may promote development of both alienation and authoritarianism, even though the two fit differing theoretical schemes. Some of the conditions, however, which give rise to alienation may be associated with nonauthoritarianism (see, for example, Warshay, Goldman, and Biddle, 1964).

The sociologist or social psychologist may find in the broad concept of alienation an explanation for authoritarianism more comfortable to deal with than the psychoanalytic theory presented in *The Authoritarian Personality*. However, the obtained relationships between alienation and authoritarianism are moderate, and the response bias factor cannot be ignored in interpretation. Second, translating alienation into authoritarianism at the conceptual or operational level is difficult. For example, several items of the dogmatism scale closely resemble items used in measuring alienation ("Most people just don't give a damn for others"), but other items diverge considerably. The possible linkage of social structure and conditions and authoritarian beliefs presents promising and exciting opportunities for future research.

V. SOCIAL PERCEPTION

Other beliefs that have been studied in relation to authoritarianism encompass descriptions of hypothetical or real persons by respondents whose F scale scores are known. Although often termed studies of "social perception," these tests actually deal with cognitive variables (i.e., the characteristics attributed to other people). In these studies the subjects provide a description of specific or hypothetical individuals (usually, as might be expected, another college student). We will examine individuals' descriptions of minority groups in the next section.

In relation to social perception, theoretical notions derived from the authoritarian personality are fairly limited. Investigators have hypothesized that authoritarianism is associated with low accuracy in judging what others are like (since authoritarian individuals presumably lack "insight" into people), greater sensitivity to certain characteristics of others (especially power), and positive evaluation of authoritarian leadership traits in others.

Much of the research used a guessing game in which the subject (selected because he scored high or low on an authoritarianism scale) filled out another F scale as he thought someone else would. This "someone else" may be either (a) a student with whom the subject talked for about 20 minutes and who was actually a high or low scoring subject, or (b) a hypothetical, typical student. Presumably, this guessing enabled the investigator to measure "accuracy" since he had actual responses available from stimulus objects.

In reality, this approach often involved invalid analyses (Cronbach, 1955) since statistical "accuracy" can be generated by characteristics of the response distributions.

Five different investigations using this technique have produced some strikingly similar results (Scodel and Mussen, 1953; Crockett and Meidinger, 1956; Rabinowitz, 1956; Scodel and Freedman, 1956; Schulberg, 1961) but little support for theoretical notions. First, in all these studies, subjects with high F scores uniformly produced a set of guesses which yielded F scores attributed to others at about the same level as their own. Low scoring persons, as a group, estimated in such a way that the attributed F scores were higher than their own. These results were obtained regardless of the actual scores of the person judged, so greater "accuracy" cannot be attributed to either group. One might be tempted to conclude that high scorers saw others as quite similar to themselves while low scorers saw others as "different" (which would be true on the average). However, Crockett and Meidinger, and Schulberg examined patterns of responses given by those guessing and those guessed about. High F subjects were no more likely than low F subjects to show high similarity to their own response pattern, and the actual response patterns of those guessed about as compared with the attributed pattern did not differ for high and low scorers. The only valid conclusion is that authoritarians and nonauthoritarians differed in the F scale responses they attributed to other people.

Schulberg used refinements which added to the nonresults: he selected consistent authoritarians and nonauthoritarians by using both original and reversed F scale items. He had subjects make judgments about both types of items and added ratings on adjectives selected to embody authoritarian characteristics. In addition to replicating the findings of others on the original F scale items, he found an opposite pattern when the items were reversals, concluding, "the present findings seem to indicate that both authoritarians and nonauthoritarians agree with what they agree (*sic*). It is only about things they oppose that they feel themselves to be isolated from others" (p. 106). The adjective ratings did not differentiate between the groups.

Authoritarians supposedly cannot appraise themselves as accurately as others, especially regarding personal failure or weakness. Niems and Scodel (1956) pointed out, however, that this inability need not require that persons scoring high on the F scale be more homogeneous in reaction to a situation requiring self-appraisal than nonauthoritarians, as often has been assumed. Their data did not support their prediction that authoritarians would give less realistic estimates of their success in a task. However, they did find that those scoring high on the F scale were more likely to shift their level of aspiration following a success or failure. These shifts were more likely to be erratic than shifts by subjects scoring low. Schulberg (1961) found no differences between consistent authoritarians and nonauthoritarians on adjective self-ratings, yet Pannes (1963) found a more favorable self-image among dogmatic subjects.

Jones (1954) asked high and low scorers on the F scale to describe a person (presented by means of a tape recording), using a prepared set of descriptive traits. There were several variations in the recording; persons presented were either forceful or passive in terms of "power" and favored either democratic or authoritarian leadership. A very complicated design and some unreliable measuring instruments produced indecisive results. Authoritarian subjects were not more "sensitive" to the power variable, nor did they show a consistently higher valuation of "authoritarian" leadership style (although they showed some tendency in this direction). They did, on the average, tend to give more favorable judgments and apparently showed less variability in their application of the traits. The more favorable descriptions given by authoritarians posed a problem, as other investigators, using scales of "misanthropy" (Sullivan and Adelson, 1954; Rosenberg, 1958), obtained results suggesting that authoritarians are misanthropes and negative about others. Perhaps authoritarians will give more "conventional" descriptions of specific people (and, generally, college students attribute favorable characteristics to others, at least if they don't know them very well), but will subscribe to negative ideology about people in general. This is, after all, in line with the manifest content of the F scale. Wrightsman (1962) demonstrated that authoritarians are aware of the extremity of their beliefs with respect to the content of the F scale.

A study by Steiner and Johnson (1963a) added an important cognitive dimension by associating scores on the F scale with a tendency to categorize people as good or bad. The authors concluded that authoritarian persons are reluctant to believe that "good people" can have both good and bad attributes.

In summary, authoritarians seem to differ from nonauthoritarians in the characteristics they attribute to others. Of the specific patterns about social perception derived from authoritarianism, there is little evidence supporting specific relationships.

VI. ETHNIC BELIEFS AND INTOLERANCE

An enormous literature exists on the subjects of prejudice, intolerance, and discrimination. Rather than trying to touch on all of these, we shall cite only illustrative studies to try to show the relationship of authoritarianism to these variables. Allport (1954) gave a comprehensive introduction to the topic of prejudice.

Concern with prejudiced attitudes, specifically antisemitism, was the original impetus for the study of authoritarianism. Intolerance, investigators theorized, was a means for dealing with psychological difficulties by converting tension into hatred for various ethnic groups. What appeared on the surface, according to this view, were negative beliefs about these groups. A distinct approach to the study of intolerance has grown up around this conception with the role of authoritarianism typically treated as a causal factor, a relatively fixed characteristic of personality, which finds one means of expression through intolerance.

Using a scale of "ethnocentrism" (the E scale) that included references to specific minority groups, the Berkeley investigators (Adorno and others, 1950) opened up an area of prolific investigation. In many studies by a variety of researchers, the E scale consistently has yielded positive relationships to the F scale, supporting the original studies. The F scale was developed as a more general measure of the personality factors underlying ethnocentrism. Methodologically, however, the relationship between the E and F scales is ambiguous (Hyman and Sheatsley, 1954). But Rokeach reported positive correlations between the E scale and his scale of dogmatism, which does not include items in common with the E scale. The problem of acquiescence may account for at least part of this result.

Of interest here are two types of findings that emerged from the personality approach to ethnic intolerance. First, some evidence suggests a general factor of prejudice; intolerance toward various minority groups tends to be interrelated. (For more discussion of this point, see the chapter on "Prejudice and Ethnic Relations," by Harding, Kutner, Proshansky, and Chein, in Lindzey, 1954.) Campbell and McCandless (1951) developed a measure of "xenophobia," which appears to be free from potential acquiescence bias.

The instrument measured reactions to several minority groups on several dimensions, such as morality and social distance. Results based on this scale yielded a general factor of intolerance which cut across the minority groups judged. In addition, the scores on xenophobia related positively to both the E scale and the F scale. Second, if measures of authoritarianism and independent measures of intolerance are free from response artifacts, the relationships found indicate that intolerence is somewhat embedded in general psychological functioning. Specifically, the F scale and the dogmatism scale make no reference to minority groups, and some studies report relationships to measures of intolerance not explained simply by acquiescence bias interpretation. For example, Siegman (1961) found in a cross-cultural study an association between prejudice and authoritarianism with the variable of differing political attitude controlled. Kutner and Gordon (1964) found that less prejudiced children performed better on tests of cognitive functioning. A followup nine years later yielded the same results. In addition, their evidence indicated that changes in cognitive functioning over time were associated with changes in prejudice.

We do not mean that a personality-based explanation of intolerance is the "real" explanation nor that it accounts for all intolerance. Rhyne (1962) gave a strong sociological explanation for prejudice, specifically rejecting the approach taken in *The Authoritarian Personality*.

Prothro (1952) reported that a large proportion of southern, white adults were anti-Negro, although they scored rather low on general ethnocentrism. In a study comparing matched communities in both the northern and southern United States, Pettigrew (1958a) found the southern sample more anti-Negro than the northern respondents, but not different on F scale scores. In another part of the same research, F scale responses of South African students were very similar to American student samples even though the South African group showed a high degree of anti-African (anti-Negro) feeling. Pettigrew concluded that social and cultural factors, rather than personality needs, explained these regional differences in ethnic intolerance. In support of his interpretation, Pettigrew found that the "culture-carriers" in the South (churchgoers, upwardly mobile respondents, and women) were more anti-Negro; that was not true in the North. On the surface, these findings do not support the idea of a general personality factor of intolerance. However, powerful cultural demands or group norms that attain the character of moral precepts may overide or mask personality dispositions.

A useful summary of the diverse functions of prejudice was prepared by Simpson and Yinger (1958). They regarded prejudice as a complex phenomenon "caused" by various types of factors, including the structure of society and the cultural norms, as well as individual values and motives. Under their theory situational and cultural factors affect learning and expression of intolerance. Also, there are many alternative ways of expressing personal anxieties and tensions, only some of which include ethnic intolerance. Some portion of intolerance, on the average, could be attributed to personality functioning. What seems lacking in this sort of analysis is an integration of the different conceptual levels, or at least an assessment of their relevance to one another.

Coming back to authoritarianism, we will examine some studies dealing with correlates of ethnocentrism. Sullivan and Adelson (1954) found that the E scale related positively to a measure of "misanthropy" (not the same, unfortunately, as Rosenberg's scale, mentioned above) with the conclusion that "for many of the anti-democratic, there may be no ingroup other than the self" (p. 247). Although one may stumble over reference to the self as an ingroup in this statement, the notion of suspicion and distrust is there. Martin and Westie (1959) found some of the same elements. Selecting tolerant and intolerant respondents from a sample of urban adults, these investigators administered a long questionnaire covering a wide range of topics. Respondents high in intolerance, as measured by a comprehensive scale which elicited opinions about Negroes, as compared to the tolerant group, had higher F scale scores. They also exhibited a higher degree of nationalism; superstition; rigid, categorical thinking; suspicion; and religiosity. Neither religious affiliation nor occupational mobility differentiated the tolerant and the intolerant groups. Although the modal income reported by the two groups did not differ, the tolerant group had a higher educational and occupational level, which may account for some of the differences in authoritarianism. The authors concluded that the original findings of *The Authoritarian Personality* were essentially valid. Although the response bias problem still was ignored, the use of adults rather than students as respondents was a welcome change.

The lack of significant results in the Martin and Westie study on occupational mobility raises some problems in comparison with results of other research. Bettelheim and Janowitz (1950) found recent shifts downward in occupational level related to intolerance toward Negroes and Jews. Long-term mobility, up or down, between manual and nonmanual occupations related positively to prejudice in an analysis of survey data by Greenblum and Pearlin (in Bendix and Lipset, 1953). Those moving either way showed more intolerance than stationary persons. The authors explained this finding as a result of "prestige insecurity" deriving from both types of mobility. The competitive social system produced strains on those involved in change, and, presumably, it focused on conventional targets of blame. However, these results depended on subjective class identification, which seems to involve personality variables to some extent.

In reanalyzing data from several national surveys that included questions on prejudice and discrimination, Stember (1961) concluded that the impact of education on intolerance is complex. In fact, certain aspects of prejudice seemed enhanced among those with more education, while other aspects were negatively related to education or showed no relationship at all. He noted that the effects of education in reducing prejudice were strongest when education separated the individual from his previous subculture (assuming that the norms of the subculture reinforced the prejudiced beliefs). According to this conclusion, not every change in status would lead to the stress-prejudice cycle suggested by Greenblum and Pearlin. More work might be done profitably on the role of various types of stress in relation to authoritarianism, both as an antecedent and as a correlate.

Kaufman (1957) found a positive relationship between a measure of "concern with status" achievement and maintenance and a scale of antisemitic beliefs. With F scale scores partialed out, the status measure still showed a significant relationship with antisemitism. Although Kaufman felt the latter result quite important, it seems equally plausible to interpret the scale of "status concern" as a measure of general intolerance as the items seem to fit this. Similarly, Srole (1956) found a moderate relationship between his measure of "anomia" ("self-to-others alienation") and both prejudice against minority groups and F scale scores. Anomia retained the relationship to prejudice with the F scale scores partialed out within socioeconomic levels. Both the Srole and Kaufman scales, however, were liable to response bias, and the findings may simply show that their scales were better measures of acquiescence than was the F scale. In content, however, both the "anomia" and "status concern" measures seem to reflect deep distrust of others.

Both Roberts and Rokeach (1956) and McDill (1961) found that "anomia" and F scale scores showed about the same relationships to prejudice (correlations between .60 and .70). Neither education nor occupational level greatly affected these relationships. Partialing out authoritarianism left a moderate relationship between anomia and prejudice, but partialing out anomia had exactly the same effect on the authoritarianism and prejudice relationship. McDill concluded that "There is a common psychological dimension underlying the three scales" (p. 245). Acquiescence may well have contaminated that dimension. McDill did a factor analysis on his data and found a general first factor which contained the highest loadings of all the anomia, authoritarianism, and prejudice items; education had a high negative loading on this factor.

Hites and Kellog (1964) reported a correlation based on 141 students from a liberal arts college in the South between F and a two-item prejudice score of minus .55. Those higher in authoritarianism generally favored segregation in schools and churches. In this study the Webster, Sanford, and Freedman scale (1955), here labeled Social Maturity but still scored for authoritarianism, yielded a correlation of minus .46 with the prejudice score.

In an unusual study treating authoritarianism and prejudice as dependent variables, Cowen, Landes, and Schaet (1959) found that mild frustration increased anti-Negro prejudice, an effect more pronounced in their male subjects than in their female subjects. Their experiment included use of prior measures of authoritarianism and prejudice, a problem-solving session in which the problems were insoluble, and followup measures with comparable but different items. F scale and E scale scores showed no change. The authors concluded that frustration augments the expression of prejudice with a specific minority group "targeted." Apparently, the effects of the frustration were too mild to produce any changes in authoritarianism.

According to Rokeach, the psychological mechanism for ethnic intolerance is based on identifying the degree to which groups are cognitively similar to oneself. It is not the outgroup as such that is rejected, but their beliefs (as perceived by the individual). Thus, Negroes are seen by intolerant whites as quite different in their belief structure, in much the same way that a dogmatic Catholic would view Baptists. Presumably, both psychological and social stress could enhance the effect. This approach provides a way of integrating the personality aspect of prejudice with the study of beliefs and attitudes in general; it may be able to do much more. Much of the evidence he presented in *The Open and Closed Mind* appears to be free from response bias interpretation.

Triandis and Triandis (1960) investigated various determinants of social distance, asking subjects to respond to hypothetical persons whose race, social class, religion, and nationality were varied systematically. Race proved the most important stimulus factor and, in addition, total social distance scores were associated with F scale scores. The authors interpreted social distance as arising from cultural norms, the resolution of cognitive dissonance, and personal insecurity. Triandis (1961) took strong exception to Rokeach's contention that perceived differences in *belief* determine social discrimination. He repeated the earlier study, adding a measure of belief similarity, and his results still singled out race as the most important determinant of discrimination. (See also Triandis, Davis, and Takezawa,

1965.) In a comment on Triandis' 1961 study, Rokeach (1961) rightly pointed out that the measure of belief utilized by Triandis was vague and not meaningful.

Subsequently, Stein, Hardyck, and Smith (1965) presented high school students with relatively detailed descriptions of peers, varying systematically the beliefs and the race of the stimulus objects. The results, based on items dealing with social distance, "strongly support Rokeach's theory that the variable of belief congruence accounts for a major portion of the variance in prejudice" (p. 289). Yet, the effects of race appeared for certain items (such as "live in the same apartment house"), suggesting that some areas of prejudice are culturally demanded. The authors concluded that subjects will use information regarding beliefs where available, but "when the belief component is not provided, spelled out in considerable detail, subjects will react in racial terms on the basis of assumptions concerning the belief systems of others, and of emotional or institutionalized factors" (p. 289).

For the theory of authoritarianism, intolerance is a key concept, but the judgmental criteria for rejection of others are not central in the theory—any learned social discrimination could function in the service of authoritarianism. Triandis has shown that cultures weight social characteristics in relation to social distance and that such characteristics (for example, race) are used in judgments about others. On the other hand, Rokeach has evidence that belief similarity may form a basic dimension in admitting others to close association.

VII. COMMENTS ON AUTHORITARIANISM AND RELATED BELIEFS

Investigators have sought, in numerous studies involving many kinds of variables, to specify beliefs that are associated with the authoritarian personality. Many of the studies have attempted to establish a consistency between content regarded as reflecting authoritarianism and some new content. Such expected consistency usually arises from consideration of a portion of the theory expressed in *The Authoritarian Personality*, or from a "logical" extension of the theory. Characteristically, authoritarianism is treated as the independent variable, determining the adherence to other beliefs.

While the many points resulting from particular studies vary, most find authoritarianism related to quite general beliefs, especially those reflecting intolerance and distrust. The more specific the dependent belief, the less likely existing measures of authoritarianism will yield a relationship (for example, with an opinion on whether foreign aid should be increased). Aside from problems of response bias, there are plausible reasons for this result. Specific beliefs arise from many different bases and through the contribution of many factors, even though an authoritarian outlook may represent a primary frame of reference. In addition, social norms strongly influence particular beliefs and their expression. The same influences would apply to specific behaviors, such as voting for a particular candidate. To add to the problem, the common assumption that authoritarianism encompasses an ideology that is both inclusive and internally consistent is untenable for the population at large. Ideology cannot be inferred from the manifest content of the F scale. These considerations suggest that the search for more correlates of authoritarianism is less worthwhile than exploration of the origin of beliefs and their meaning within an authoritarian framework (see Smith, Bruner, and White, 1956).

In the area of ethnic intolerance the F scale relates best to specific content. That is not surprising since the scale was developed to measure prejudice indirectly. However, even in the study of prejudice, the concept of authoritarianism must be integrated further with other levels and types of explanation. Here (and in other areas as well) social factors have great relevance to the study of the authoritarian personality. Such factors represent, first, a set of conditions under which the development of authoritarianism is or is not likely; second, they affect the opportunity for formation and expression of various beliefs; third, they are relevant to the concept of alienation and its relationship to the development or expression of authoritarian behavior. A more adequate theoretical structure for authoritarianism would encompass both social and psychological variables. A formulation of this sort concerning the development of authoritarianism has been outlined by Kelman and Barclay (1963).

It seems curious that research on authoritarianism has been directed toward specific beliefs, such as socialized medicine. In particular, the way in which beliefs are treated often is puzzling. In social psychology today probably the major theories of belief and attitude are functional theories (for example, see Smith, Bruner, and White, 1956; Katz and Stotland, 1959) which treat attitudes as closely tied with the individual's values and motives. The psychological meaning of the attitude depends on the cognitive structure in which it is embedded. There is no reason to suppose that every belief serves the same type of function for an authoritarian person, nor that a given belief serves an authoritarian purpose. The role of belief in context has often been disregarded and unexplored, partly because of the misplaced zeal for objective-looking scales. A major contribution by Rokeach lies in his emphasis on structural aspects of cognitive functioning in contrast to manifest content. Pettigrew (1961) made the point that research on desegregation has not exploited fully the concept of attitude; that point seems to apply more generally to research on authoritarianism.

Social Behavior
and Authoritarianism

Some of the most interesting social psychological research on the topic of authoritarianism deals with its effects on interaction with others and ways it influences various aspects of group behavior. Characteristically, authoritarianism is treated as a fixed disposition of an individual, affecting his interaction with others and having consequences for group processes and products. In some cases authoritarianism itself is considered a dependent variable. Many of the studies, including a number of laboratory experiments, provide data free from acquiescence response bias.

We have divided studies discussed in this section into four groups based on the conception of authoritarianism underlying the research efforts. First, we consider studies dealing with a change in attitudes in which authoritarianism is considered representative of deep-seated and irrational attachment to particular beliefs. These studies, generally narrow in scope, show a functionalist approach to attitude structure and change. Second, we discuss studies which attempt to specify social-situational components which support or modify authoritarian dispositions. These studies generally attempt to relate membership in primary groups to authoritarianism. Third, we examine studies which explore the effects of authoritarianism in individuals on behavior in groups, usually small, problem-solving laboratory groups. Finally, we will consider studies on authoritarianism and organizational roles, focusing on both leadership and complex organizations.

Some remarks about the background of these studies are necessary. At the theoretical level, what is the relevance of authoritarianism to social behavior? Examination of the dimensions forming the conceptual basis of authoritarianism (say, in *The Authoritarian Personality*) yields various implications of attitudes and actions toward others which would be consistent with this personality syndrome. In fact, most of the research reported below represents an extrapolation from descriptions of the authoritarian person presented by the Berkeley investigators. An implicit formulation of behaviors consistent with personality factors rather than a rigorous development of theory or system of interrelated hypotheses has guided much of the research. For example, the conceptual notion that authoritarian persons are preoccupied with dominance-submission aspects of interpersonal relations generated hypotheses about behavior in groups. In group tasks more authoritarian persons, it has been argued, would be disruptive under cooperative forms of interaction, under "democratic" modes of distributing responsibility, and under "non-directive" styles of leadership. Rigidity in approach to the solution of problems might also be expected. In terms of those behaviors which maintain the group (for example, expressions of cohesiveness), investigators have regarded authoritarianism as potentially disruptive in groups with members both high and low on authoritarianism; the authoritarian member might be expected to show more preoccupation with his status in the group. Conformity in relation to authoritarianism has received attention because the authoritarian person is regarded as anxious to conform to the expectations of others, especially if those others are powerful. These are some of the notions which have guided research on authoritarianism and social behavior.

I. ATTITUDE CHANGE THROUGH PERSUASION

Repression and projective mechanisms form a basic component in the concept of the authoritarian personality; negative beliefs about oneself or others in positions of authority are repressed and subsequently projected onto nonthreatening entities, such as members of minority groups. Several authors suggested the need for tailoring an appeal for attitude change to the predominant motivational base of the attitude (Sarnoff and Katz, 1954; Wagman, 1955; Smith, Bruner, and White, 1956; Katz and Stotland, 1959). If the primary function served by an attitude is projection, displacement, or "scapegoating," then rational appeals directed at the content of the attitude itself will not be effective. If the attitude serves such functions, then providing "insight" regarding the personality dynamics of the prejudiced belief might lead to attitude change in the direction advocated. A series of studies by Katz and his associates investigated this problem using all or part of the F scale to measure defensiveness.

Katz, McClintock, and Sarnoff (1957) predicted that persons with a moderate amount of defensiveness would show more attitude change following administration of material designed to produce insight than would those high in defensiveness, because the high defensives would be too rigid to respond to the influence or would feel too threatened by it. Investigators also theorized that those low in defensiveness should change relatively little because defensiveness did not form the basis of their attitude. To provide insight, the subject read a long passage that explained relationships between emotions and attitudes, describing such mechanisms as scapegoating, compensation, and projection. In short, the authors asked subjects to learn some theory. Certain clusters of items from the F scale measured ego-defensiveness, including authoritarian aggression, anti-intraception, superstition and stereotypy, destructiveness and cynicism, projectivity, and sex. The remaining sections of the F scale, measuring conventionalism, authoritarian submission, and power and toughness, were used as a conformity scale. Those with intermediate scores on the defensiveness measure changed more in the direction of favorable attitudes toward Negroes in the course of the study than did those scoring high on the scale. Those low in defensiveness evidenced a degree of change between that of other groups.

McClintock (1958), using similar techniques and procedures, reported comparable findings. A third similar study (Stotland, Katz, and Patchen, 1959) yielded contradictory findings that among prejudiced subjects those low in defensiveness changed more than the moderately defensive individuals; as expected, the moderate group changed more than the high defensive subjects. As the authors stated, this result may have been due to the "absolute" amount of ego-defensiveness in the subjects who were low relative to others studied, or to a wrong prediction, or to use of the F scale as the measure of ego-defensiveness.

The major dependent variable in the studies mentioned was a measure of attitudes toward Negroes, consisting of 15 anti-Negro and six pro-Negro statements on a questionnaire. The pro-Negro items, included to avoid response bias, were interspersed throughout the form. The attitude changes obtained in these studies cannot be accounted for by acquiescence, however. Those subjects who changed most were prejudiced (i.e., gave many "agree" responses to the 15-item Negro stereotype scale) and were medium or low on the measure of ego-defense (i.e., tended to give "disagree" responses to the F scale items).

As another measure of ego-defensiveness, Katz, McClintock, and Sarnoff (1957) administered the "Paranoid" scale of the Minnesota Multiphasic Personality Inventory. Scores on this scale related highly to the F scale measures of ego-defensiveness and yielded similar results following attempts at persuasion. In the data reported by Couch and Keniston (1960), scores on the "Paranoid" scale were little affected by agreement response bias.

There is the danger in these studies that the actual change occurred in the instrumental value of the attitude for the subject in maintaining his self-defining relationship to others, rather than the ego-defensive aspect of attitudes. Thus, after reading the material designed to provide insight, the individual may have thought it appropriate to express less prejudice than before because the experimenters seemed to require a more tolerant attitude. This is not a question of simple acquiescence, however. A recent study by Sherman (1965), partly replicating the McClintock study, suggested that these "demand characteristics" of the experimental situation may explain some of the changes observed.

Wagman (1955) incorporated theoretically interesting features involving varied reactions to attempts at changing attitudes. Based on the rationale presented by Sarnoff and Katz (1954), Wagman used a "cognitive restructuring" (information) technique, which he predicted would be more effective for persons low on authoritarianism. He also attempted change by authoritarian suggestion, predicting that this technique would produce more change among those relatively more authoritarian. In one condition, the authoritarian suggestion called for more tolerant attitudes; in the other condition, the authoritarian statement suggested more prejudice. Thus, Wagman could assess the effect of authoritarian suggestion when its direction opposed the "natural tendencies" of the authoritarian subject. The results confirmed that the informational approach was more effective in attitude change among those low in authoritarianism. Furthermore, when the more authoritarian subjects received the same information, they changed their opinions in the *opposite* direction. Authoritarian suggestion supporting prejudice also affected the two groups differently, with the authoritarian subjects moving toward more prejudice and the nonauthoritarians becoming less prejudiced. Under authoritarian suggestion to become less prejudiced, there was no differential change between the two groups; rather, both groups became somewhat less prejudiced, a change in the direction of the influence. Thus, the informational technique yielded more tolerant response from those low in authoritarianism while those higher in authoritarianism changed opposite to the intended effect. An authoritative suggestion that the subjects become less tolerant had the intended effect on authoritarians but not on nonauthoritarians.

This change cannot be attributed to response bias because persons with high scores on the F scale (presumably reflecting a disposition to agree with authoritative-sounding statements) also should have changed their attitude in the direction the experimenters seemed to require. Although those scoring low on the F scale (i.e., not acquiescing) in general did not change in the direction of the suggestion (they were affected in the direction of the suggestion in only one case), the more authoritarian group changed, when given information, in a direction opposite to that intended. Nothing in the theory of response bias would account for such a change.

It is probably significant that the beliefs chosen by the investigators in these studies of persuasion concerned intolerance. If the findings on changes in belief are valid, we might ask to what range of topics they apply. Theoretically, only those beliefs linked with authoritarianism should be affected, but we do not know, on the average, how strongly authoritarian dispositions affect different items in an individual's cognitive systems. Perhaps only "central" beliefs are involved. In terms of persuasion, the attempts of experimenters to create insight had little effect on authoritarian subjects. Even among those affected, reading a psychological explanation of the dynamics of prejudice will not create any lasting effect, unless the reading is supported outside the experimental situation. It appears, however, that authoritarian suggestion does have potential value for attitude change among authoritarian subjects (and this finding agrees with Rokeach's discussion of "party-line thinking" in *The Open and Closed Mind*). Such persuasion apparently is potent because it also has side effects on nonauthoritarians.

Harvey and Beverly (1961) found that a message attributed to a high status source produced more attitude change among subjects scoring high on authoritarianism. Low scorers changed more when the source of the message was presented as anonymous. In a second test condition, Harvey and Beverly asked subjects to provide arguments for the point of view contained in the source's message, manipulating the message so that the point of view it contained was the opposite of that held by the subject. Under these circumstances both the low and high authoritarian subjects showed more change regardless of whether the source was given or not. Harvey and Beverly used the Webster measure of authoritarianism for their research. Using politics and candidates as subject matter, Powell (1962) found closed-minded respondents unable to differentiate between the content of a message and its source.

II. GROUP MEMBERSHIP AND AUTHORITARIANISM

Several studies have found group membership and authoritarianism related. In a unique field experiment Siegel and Siegel (1957) examined changes in F scale scores of freshman girls as a consequence of their living arrangements at a university and their desire over a period of one year to live in high status groups, characterized as more authoritarian. At the beginning of the study, high scorers on an adaptation of the E and F scales were asked their choice of living group, and all who chose the high status groups remained in the study. Based on their knowledge of the different living arrangements, the authors hypothesized that the high status groups would maintain a relatively authoritarian set of norms. Under normal university procedure, freshman girls were assigned randomly to a living group. The random assignment is a crucial factor in the forcefulness of the results of the study. After a year preferences for living groups were again collected, and the F scale was readministered. Theoretically, all girls held the high status, authoritarian groups as reference groups at the outset, although none of the girls was yet a member of these groups. At the end of the study, the high status groups were both reference groups and membership groups for the girls who had been assigned there. These high status groups were also reference groups, but not membership groups, for those girls assigned to lower status living groups but who, after a year, still aspired to the higher status groups. For the girls who lived in the lower status groups and came to prefer them, the higher status groups were neither reference nor membership groups. Because a reference group generally influences relevant opinions and attitudes (F scale scores), the investigators expected the latter group of girls to become less authoritarian and the other two groups to remain the same. The data showed that girls whose reference group had changed became less authoritarian as measured by the F scale. Unexpectedly, the girls whose membership groups were lower status (less authoritarian) also became less authoritarian, although they still preferred the higher status, more authoritarian groups. Of special interest here is the use of authoritarianism as a dependent variable, influenced by social attachments and norms.

In an exploratory study lacking in controls, Wells, Chiaravallo, and Goldman (1957) obtained ratings by members in five different social fraternities, covering topics such as the intellectual emphasis of the fraternity, amount of public humiliation demanded of those seeking membership, and the various barriers to membership based on race and religion. From these ratings the authors ranked the five fraternities on something like "intolerance." Actual scores on authoritarianism, obtained from members, corresponded fairly well to the ranking. It is not clear whether authoritarianism was antecedent or consequent (or both) to membership in the group; both selection of members and group norms, plus other factors, could have been at work.

A study by Aumack (1955) found that San Quentin inmates serving time for first degree murder exhibited the highest F scale scores recorded as of that date. His study focused on (a) the dimensions of authoritarianism emerging when F scale scores of such a group of convicts are cluster analyzed and (b) the relationship between scores on the F scale and scores based on the obtained clusters, on the one hand, and length of time in prison, on the other. The clusters obtained were not parallel to either the components of authoritarianism specified by Adorno and his associates (1950) or to the empirical categories reported by Christie and Garcia (1951). Further, no consistent patterns of authoritarianism appeared as a function of length of imprisonment.

Another study of prisoners by Grusky (1962) determined the degree to which prison indoctrination was successful. According to the author, acceptance of indoctrination by a "member" of the organization depended on the organization's authority structure, the subculture of the members, and the member's predilections for authority. Grusky's formulation led to the notion that, in a "treatment-oriented" prison (as opposed to a traditional prison), the authority structure is more consistent with the norms of the member, and the authoritarian prisoners would be more likely to accept indoctrination from the prison officials. He used F scale scores to classify the prisoners into high and low authoritarian groups. On a variety of measures—including attitudes toward the prison camp and the treatment program, amount of participation in activities, and overall adjustment—the more authoritarian prisoners showed relatively greater acceptance of the prison program. The results, although of considerable interest in the light of the conceptual scheme, were weakened by the lack of control groups and evidence of change over time. Authoritarianism, in this case, was treated as a variable conditioning the relationship between influence attempts and beliefs, but the extent to which selection and situational factors affected the results was not clear.

Three other studies exploring the effects of group membership on authoritarianism did not yield the expected results. Jones (1956) considered imprisonment an indicator of exposure to a group expected to produce more authoritarian beliefs. A group of navy retrainees who had been in prison was compared with a group of nondelinquent trainees. A special measure of authoritarianism employed did not show a very strong relationship to F scale scores. Although the two groups differed in measured authoritarianism in the expected direction, the difference disappeared with the introduction of a control for differences in scholastic aptitude scores. In another study, Campbell and McCormack (1957) retested Air Force officer cadets on F scale items after a year in the service. They expected an increase in authoritarianism, stemming from the respondents' experience as members of the military organization. Retesting showed a significant *reduction* in scores over the year's time. Solomon (1963) found changes toward less authoritarianism from subjects high on authoritarianism both in groups composed of author- itarian members and in mixed groups, interpreting the find- ings as a result of deference to authority.

The studies outlined in this section present mixed results. Group membership is important for the support and modifi- cation of beliefs, but variables such as the manner of selec- tion into groups and the consistency between individual dispositions and group standards must be considered in assessing such effects. As is the case with relationships between various beliefs and authoritarianism described pre- viously, membership in particular natural groups does not necessarily create or change authoritarian dispositions. The most promising aspects of the studies are in the evidence that authoritarian beliefs may be modified socially and in the tie between the structure and functioning of beliefs and their social context. In spite of the ambiguities in findings, the research noted here has touched on questions of great importance: the role of membership groups in creating or modifying the authoritarian personality and the importance of the social ecology in its maintenance. Investigators have tended to look at total institutions, such as prisons or the military because of their obvious importance, yet other types of groups can provide significant experiences. Another side of the problem is the question of self-selection into groups which maintain personality dispositions and provide a congenial social reality.

III. SMALL GROUP BEHAVIOR

Over the past few years, the study of small groups has become a specialized area of social science and, in large part, a unique province of the social psychologist. Two practical orientations are prominent. First, the small group may be regarded as a miniature replica or approximation of society and the social order; the behavior of people in small groups reflects a significant portion of the actual social realm. Second, the small group as a unit of study bears close ties to certain aspects of the real world. What people do in everyday life very often involves small groups—whether family, work groups, committees, or sets of friends. Many small group theories exist, ranging from the purely psychological to the purely sociological. Often enough, however, investigators treat the psychological dispositions of the group members as one determinant of group behavior (for example, in Bass, 1960). It is in this context that we will discuss authoritarianism.

In using the concept of authoritarianism in group studies, investigators principally sought to explore the effect of a personality characteristic on social interaction. Some sought to describe how authoritarian or nonauthoritarian persons behave in a social setting; others investigated the impact of the authoritarian personality on group problem-solving processes. In these and other instances, the question is the effect a personality characteristic has on social behavior; overt, social outcomes of authoritarianism have been put to the test.

Differences in the behavior of authoritarian and nonauthoritarian members of small, problem-solving groups were described by Haythorn, Couch, Haefner, Langham, and Carter (1956). Each group consisted of four persons with homogeneous scores on the F scale (either high or low). As gauged by observers' ratings, the more authoritarian subjects tended to be more aggressive and less friendly than the less authoritarian group members. In general, though, the observations did not differentiate the two types of groups. Records of actual interaction, however, demonstrated that the nonauthoritarian subjects displayed more positive emotion, more agreement, more concern for the feelings of others, and made fewer directive acts or commands. Authoritarian members engaged more in "self-isolating" acts. Their results indicated that authoritarian dispositions may eventuate in less contribution to the group, especially in maintaining relationships among the members.

Zagona and Zurcher (1964) conducted an observational study of the behavior of dogmatic and nondogmatic undergraduates. Using scores on the dogmatism scale, they assigned 30 high scorers to one discussion section of a psychology course and 30 low scorers to another. Throughout the term, the instructors observed behavior in the two sections and over that period of time, clearcut differences appeared. The dogmatic subjects preferred lecture to discussion, and objective, structured examinations. They showed greater dependence on the instructor and more anxiety and compulsive behavior. In addition, the investigators conducted two small experiments in which groups from each of the sections met for discussions of controversial topics. Again, the behaviors exhibited by the dogmatic subjects fit expectations. For example, where the instructor challenged a consensus reached by a dogmatic group, the agreement disappeared; this did not happen in the nondogmatic group.

While the description of behavior in the two groups was

valuable, the authors reported no objective measures to bolster their observations. Nor is it clear whether observers perceiving the differences in behavior were unaware of the composition of the group. In addition, control for factors such as intellectual achievement or college major would have been desirable. However, this study suggests some exciting possibilities for future research.

In an imaginative and methodologically sophisticated study Deutsch (1960) compared subjects with high and low F scale scores in their performance in a two person game designed to test how much a subject trusted his partner and how trustworthy the subject himself was. Maximum gain was possible with a mixture of trusting and untrustworthy responses. Subjects with low F scale scores tended to be both trusting and trustworthy, while the more authoritarian subjects were more suspicious and untrustworthy. Deutsch interpreted the effects of authoritarianism in his study as signifying the influence of a personality variable on cooperative group behavior, with implications for the successful performance and maintenance of the group.

In the area of conformity and influence, several investigators have examined the relationship of authoritarianism to pressures from group members toward change, assuming as a general hypothesis that authoritarianism includes a relatively high degree of susceptibility to attempts at influencing a person. Crutchfield (1955), Canning and Baker (1959), and Nadler (1959) found tendencies toward greater conformity among their more authoritarian subjects, employing the F scale (in Nadler's case, a portion of it) as the measure of authoritarianism. In all three cases, the critical behavior involved judgments about materials visually presented. Crutchfield's "groups" involved the presence of others whose judgments, as presented to the subject, were faked by the investigator. The Canning and Baker study used more direct personal influence. Nadler announced bogus group judgments to his subjects. Wells, Weinert, and Rubel (1956) created a situation in which college students made judgments about a traffic accident with stooges pressuring half the subjects to blame the "wrong" driver. Those who were swayed under pressure had higher F scale scores than those who did not yield. Lasky (1962) reported that a group of students with high F scale scores changed their responses upon retest more than low scorers when told that their peers scored in the opposite direction. Centers and Horowitz (1963) reported a positive relationship between F scale scores and a measure of "other-directedness."

Starting with the assumption that relationships between F scale scores and measures of conformity may be confounded by general acquiescence, Vaughan and White (1966) selected groups of students who showed consistent conforming responses on three different measures and obtained scores on a forced-choice version of the F scale (Berkowitz and Wolkon, 1964). They found that conformity was associated with higher scores on authoritarianism and that each aspect of conformity measured made some independent contribution. Acquiescence alone could not account for these results.

According to these findings, the authoritarian person is more ready to yield to social pressures. Yet other investigators have failed to find differences in conformity between high and low scorers on the F scale (Hoffman, 1957; Weiner and McGinnies, 1961; Steiner and Vannoy, 1966). Since a variety of experimental situations have been used, it is difficult to reconcile the findings. Steiner and Vannoy point out that there may be a variety of conforming behaviors with different psychological meanings; they also suggest that the authoritarian may yield readily to situational demands with little change in private beliefs. Studies of conformity may lose sight of the rationale behind the hypothesized relationship between authoritarianism and conforming—the strong needs for dependence on and fear of authority. In laboratory procedures, the manipulation of social pressure may not engage these needs, or other factors in the situation may override them. There are also potential defenses against actual conformity behavior, such as denial or distortion.

Steiner and Johnson (1963b) introduced variations in the conformity situation itself. Their subjects were confronted with two confederates of the investigators in what appeared to be three person groups. In one condition, the confederates almost always agreed on a series of judgments (the actual subject made his judgment last). In a second condition, the confederates disagreed most of the time. In the third treatment, there were moderate number of disagreements between the stooges. Where the subjects faced unanimity, F scale scores related moderately to overall conformity. Faced with a high degree of disagreement between the confederates, subjects with high F scale scores usually rejected one of the confederates and conformed to the judgments of the other. In the third condition, high F scorers conformed equally to the other two "subjects." The authors formulated a differentiated view of conformity in relation to authoritarianism—authoritarian people judge others as all good or all bad and put them into ingroups or outgroups accordingly. *Conformity* to others depends on whether they are seen as both good and in agreement; otherwise, authoritarianism and conformity would show little relationship. In the Weiner and McGinnies (1961) study when the two confederates disagreed, subjects showed "almost a 50-50 split" in their responses, but low F subjects agreed significantly more often with the confederate sitting nearest the ambiguous stimulus.

Consideration of influence source further differentiates the

conformity-authoritarianism relationship. An important theoretical feature of the dogmatic individual is the lack of
distinction between the source and the content of a communication (Rokeach, 1960; see also the article by Rokeach in
Berg and Bass, 1961). In situations involving "social reality,"
the power of others has proved a particularly effective
determinant of conformity for the authoritarian person.
Berkowitz and Lundy (1957) used two "sources" of influence
on three attitude issues—the reported responses of peers and
of military leaders. After the subjects, who were all college
students, gave their own responses on the three issues, they
received the faked information and then were retested. The
influence operated in a complex way. Highly authoritarian
subjects who were also low on a measure of self-confidence
were affected by both sources; those with high self-confidence were more influenced by the information from the
military than from peers. In fact, they were more distant
from the peer position after the influence attempt, indicating
that conformity may be a complicated matter. In this study,
those with high F scale scores showed no more general
susceptibility to influence than subjects with lower scores.

Vidulich and Kaiman (1961) examined relationships between dogmatism and conformity. They selected students
on the basis of scores on the dogmatism scale choosing 30
with high scores and 30 with low scores. Subjects made
visual judgments in the presence of another "subject," who
was actually a confederate of the investigators. To half the
subjects this confederate was presented as a high status
person (a professor), and to the other half as a low status
person (a high school student). The more dogmatic group
of subjects agreed more with the high status person.

Findings from an important study of contrived biracial
groups have added some puzzling questions to the study of
behavioral manifestations of authoritarianism (Katz and

111

Benjamin, 1960). They set up four person groups, each composed of two white and two Negro college students. The group members were matched on intelligence. The study used different combinations of group *vs.* individual reward and high *vs.* neutral group prestige. To create high prestige, groups were told that they performed very well. Investigators assigned subjects to the groups on the basis of F scale scores so that half of the groups had two white high scorers and half two white low scorers. Each group met several times and worked on a variety of tasks. Researchers also obtained measures of communication, social influence, productivity, and social perception.

How did authoritarian group members react to their Negro coworkers? The results suggested greater acceptance of the Negroes by subjects with high F scale scores than those with low scores. For example, on a task requiring a high degree of cooperation, the authoritarian subjects accepted more suggestions from Negroes; they showed more compliance in group decisions; they rated the Negroes as higher on intelligence and maturity. These effects were most pronounced in the high prestige groups. No evidence of ethnocentric behavior appeared in the situations studied.

Several explanations of the results are possible. One is that lacking an independent measure of prejudice, F scale scores did not make a good measure of ethnocentrism. Another is that the F scale does not predict behavior well (see Berg, 1966). Katz and Benjamin, however, interpreted their findings as reflecting authoritarian conformity in a situation where the power figures (i.e., the investigators) obviously expected equalitarian behavior and where overt demonstration of prejudice would be punished. While this interpretation seems a good one, the efforts of authoritarian members to appear unprejudiced are surprising. It would follow that authoritarianism increases susceptibility to situational conformity in conflicts between situational constraints and response tendencies. The creation and resolution of those conflicts deserve further investigation.

Some support for the Katz and Benjamin interpretation comes from a study by Epstein (1966). Subjects were given the opportunity to shock a Negro victim following a series of shocks delivered to the victim by a fellow subject who was actually an accomplice of the investigator. This accomplice, played by a Negro for half the subjects and by a white for the other half, served as an aggressive model. More authoritarian subjects (as measured by the F scale) delivered significantly more shock and showed generalization of aggression across models. Apparently, the model served to lower barriers to aggression. Unexpectedly, those low on authoritarianism were more imitative of the Negro than the white model, suggesting that the perception of intragroup hostility is an important determinant of aggressive behavior toward a group.

Although we noted previously that sensitivity of authoritarian people to differences in power has not been demonstrated in forming impressions of others, the following studies demonstrate that status is a determinant of response selection. Thibaut and Riecken (1955) set up a two person task in which a confederate of the investigators frustrated the subject, who rated his partner before and after the task. All subjects were in a Reserve Officers Training Corps program, and the status variable was high or low rank attributed to the confederate. Facing a higher status partner, authoritarian subjects changed from the first to the second rating toward less rejection of their partner. Facing a lower status partner, they increased in rejection. Furthermore, the intensity of aggressive remarks to a lower status partner increased with authoritarianism; that relationship did not hold with higher status persons. Using a set of pictures similar to the

Rosenzweig Picture Frustration Test, Roberts and Jessor (1958) scored the degree of punitiveness expressed by subjects varying in authoritarianism. Half of the pictures presented the person responsible for the frustration as high in status (by means of attributed age, education, occupation, and income). Although the high and low authoritarian groups showed no overall difference in punitive remarks, the more authoritarian subjects responded with personal punitiveness to low status people more often than to high status people. Second, all subjects responded more often with nonpersonal punitiveness (displacement) to high rather than to low status people, but the more authoritarian group showed a higher incidence of such responses. The authors remarked that punitiveness is not a general tendency of authoritarianism alone but depends also on situational cues.

Harvey (1962) reported results which focus on the psychological nature of reactions to different sources. When confronted with ratings of themselves, supposedly given by a friend, more authoritarian subjects showed stronger resistance to changing their own ratings where a discrepancy existed; they did not devalue the friend. However, authoritarianism was associated with distortion in recall of the discrepancies. Harvey concluded that the resistance to change was characteristic of authoritarianism in relation to ego-involved objects and beliefs.

Another line of research concerns the effectiveness and morale of groups as related to the individual members' personalities. Schutz's (1955) carefully worked-out study of group productivity illustrates the approach. Schutz hypothesized that productivity varied with compatibility of group members in their psychological orientation to one another. This orientation may be based on either power considerations or personal relationships with the power orientation identified as closely related to authoritarianism.

Using group problem-solving situations, Schutz put together compatible (members shared the same orientation) and incompatible (members differed in their orientation) groups. On problems requiring cooperative solutions, the compatible groups performed better; furthermore, members preferred to work with others who shared their orientation. In the studies by Haythorn and others (1956b) with groups constructed of the different combinations of authoritarian and nonauthoritarian leaders and followers, the members felt more secure and experienced less conflict in groups homogeneous on authoritarianism. Also, observers rated the homogeneous groups as more productive and more satisfied.

These studies imply that authoritarianism has no direct bearing on task effectiveness. In a review of studies predicting group effectiveness from characteristics of members, Heslin (1964) reached the same conclusion. "In summary, four studies indicate that authoritarianism, as a unitary concept, is unrelated to small group productivity, especially under conditions of high organization where little latitude exists for personality variation to have a great influence on performance procedures," he wrote (p. 253).

The studies mentioned have attempted to specify some factors in group processes affected by authoritarian dispositions. For example, the conformity response seems to vary with specific content and source of influence. Two possible extraneous (and related) factors create problems in interpretation. First, indirect acquiescence response bias is possible. Although the behaviors studied in the research cited are free from overt acquiescence, dispositions toward response bias do not exist in a vacuum; the findings may represent correlates of agreeing response tendencies which would affect both F scale scores and other overt behaviors (this point is presented in detail by Quinn, 1963). Second, much of the research involves selection of subjects by scores on a measure of authoritarianism. A true experiment is not possible in these circumstances because the investigator, lacking control over that part of the situation, must take whatever accompanies high or low scores on his measure.

IV. LEADERSHIP, COMPLEX ORGANIZATIONS, AND AUTHORITARIANISM

In this section we will review a group of loosely related studies concerning effects of authoritarianism on leader-follower relations and interactions among personality, role, and organization. In relation to the previous sections the studies reported here deal with consequences of authoritarianism in structured social situations involving role differences. In these studies leadership is treated as a role within an organized collection of people. Also, we will discuss studies on formal organizations.

The area of leadership is still confusing. Writers have made extensive use of the authoritarian label without much concern for examining the similarities to, and differences from, the personality concept. Although authoritarian versus democratic styles of leadership have been emphasized (see the chapter by Gibb on "Leadership," in Lindzey, 1954; Bennis, 1959), much of the research and writing relates to authoritarianism as treated here principally by analogy. Useful on this point is the review by Anderson (1959) of studies comparing authoritarian and democratic styles of teaching. Our chief interest, however, is in research on personality and social psychological variables, including authoritarianism in leader or follower roles and organizational climate.

Haythorn and his colleagues (1956a) found that leaders who emerged in groups composed of members with low F scale scores as rated by observers showed more sensitivity to other members, exhibited more leadership qualities, and appeared more goal-oriented than their counterparts in high scoring groups. The groups were, of course, created in the laboratory. In a second study also using four person laboratory groups, the experimenters appointed leaders with high or low scores on the F scale; the group members consisted of either high or low scorers, representing all four possible group compositions (Haythorn and others, 1956b). Observers rated the more authoritarian leaders as more autocratic and less concerned with group approval. (Observers did not know the composition of the group they were rating.) Among the followers, those with high F scale scores appeared less equalitarian, less sensitive to others, and, interestingly, more satisfied than the low scorers with appointed leaders, even though in half the groups this leader was a low scorer. However, they did not appear more submissive to the appointed leaders, a finding which is relevant to the relationship between conformity and status differences mentioned previously. Under leaders with low scores on the F scale, the followers had more influence on group processes, but did not show more differences of opinion in relation to the group tasks. In groups with followers who had scored low, both types of leaders exhibited less autocratic behavior and less assertive leadership. Thus, personality variables interacted with the composition of the group. At least in the area of small groups, these two studies represent the best information available on the relationship between authoritarianism and leadership.

Bass and his coworkers (1953) rated the leadership status attained in a group discussion situation. The groups started off without leaders. There was a low negative relationship between rated leadership and scores on the F scale, but the relationship was not linear. Although subjects with high scores on the F scale scored somewhat poorly on leadership, those with low scores also seemed to be relatively poor. The authors concluded that emergent leaders are less stereotyped, less submissive, less power-oriented, and less rigid than nonleaders. Mowry (1957) reported the development of an objective test of "supervisory insight," which, with a sample of 40 supervisors in a chemical plant, showed a moderate negative relationship to scores on the F scale. These studies suggested that authoritarianism may decrease the probability of an individual's selection as a leader, although situational constraints undoubtedly play a part.

Medalia (1955) conducted a relatively elaborate study on the acceptance of a formal leader, investigating a theory of group cohesion. Starting with the premise that cohesion is a function of the members' personalities, Medalia predicted that authoritarianism would be associated with high acceptance of formal leaders, especially where strong sanctions were available. Where the leaders are sharply differentiated in status and power, groups with more authoritarian members would also exhibit a high degree of cohesion, he predicted. The subjects were actual groups of U. S. Air Force enlisted men, giving the author a situation involving both clearcut status and strong sanctions. In addition to scores on an abbreviated F scale, the study used a question on reenlistment intention to measure cohesiveness, and, peculiarly, a set of items dealing with the leader's "human relations mindedness" to measure leader acceptance. For the various groups of men (averages for groups constituted the scores), an overall relationship between authoritarianism and both leader acceptance and group cohesion was evident. The relationship, however, did not exist in groups with either high or low scores on the F scale, but only in those with medium scores. The author had difficulty explaining this result, suggesting that both high and low scoring groups were "rigid." The adequacy of the measuring instruments must be questioned, and, in addition, the importance of the relationship between the norms of the group members and the formal organization should not be overlooked. Grusky (1962) discusses the latter point. No conclusive evidence that formal leaders are more accepted by authoritarian individuals has yet been found.

The concept of authoritarianism has been included in several organizational studies. Researchers have studied some effects of authoritarianism on formal organizations and its relationship to various aspects of organizational functioning, although their findings are fragmentary.

In an industrial organization Vroom and Mann (1960) found that certain aspects of workers' satisfaction with their jobs related to authoritarianism in their supervisors. In some work groups the authoritarianism of the supervisor (measured by F scale scores) related negatively to the workers' satisfaction with the supervisor and the overall work situation. In other work groups the relationships were positive. In the latter groups the workers actually saw more authoritarian supervisors as exerting less pressure, creating less tension, and providing more participation. The groups of workers did not differ on measured authoritarianism in a way that could explain the findings, but the groups did vary in size, as was noted after the fact, with more satisfaction expressed for authoritarian supervisors in larger groups. According to the authors, these groups displayed less interdependence and lower interaction among the group members. The tasks of the larger and smaller groups, however, also differed. Structural variables may have mediated the relationship between satisfaction with supervisors and authoritarian supervision; or, the behavior of the supervisors may not have reflected the authoritarianism attributed to them.

As part of the same study, Vroom (1958; 1959) examined the relationship between authoritarianism and participation in decision-making among 108 supervisors. Participation was measured by the respondents' answers to questionnaire items, such as the amount of influence exerted by the respondent on his superior. The author predicted that experience of participation would be negatively valued by authoritarian individuals, leading to dissatisfaction and poor performance on the job. Conversely, greater participation should produce both satisfaction and performance for non-authoritarian persons. Vroom found participation positively related to job satisfaction, and the relationship varied with the degree of authoritarianism. He found the highest relationship for the supervisors with low scores on the F scale, but found no relationship for high scorers (the results would have been more striking had this relationship been negative). In addition, degree of participation and performance on the job, as measured by ratings, correlated positively for the group with low F scale scores, but not for the high scorers. Vroom concluded that authoritarian personality dispositions mediated the effects of participation on the motivation for effective performance on the job. To a large extent, the framework for more or less participation is set by the structure and culture of the organization or of constituent groups.

Another example of the relationship of authoritarianism to interpersonal relations is an extensive study of organizational stress concerned with personality factors involved in role conflict and ambiguity (Kahn and others, 1964). Both interview and questionnaire materials were obtained from a variety of role occupants in seven different companies. Factor analysis of the questionnaire information yielded a dimension of flexibility-rigidity. The authors characterized the rigid person as inner-directed, dogmatic, and authoritarian in interpersonal relationships. From interview material, the rigid organizational member appeared to be highly accepting of and dedicated to responsibilities assigned by organizational authorities. He typically got into conflict from unquestioning acceptance of too much work from superiors or through strict adherence to internalized standards. On the other hand, they found that the more flexible person was more often exposed to conflict because of openness to influence and attempts to please others. Given the strong orientation to status and authority, the rigid person conforms more to rules and is quite dependable; yet he is less open to influence and, particularly under conflict, rejects his equals or subordinates as role senders. While the findings did not stem directly from the usual measures of authoritarianism, they are of particular interest because of the organizational scope of the study and the valuable information concerning personality functioning in a real-life job setting.

The study on fraternity groups by Wells, Chiaravallo, and Goldman (1957) was described previously. They found that ratings on the authoritarian climate of the groups corresponded with average F scale scores for the members. Much more intensive work on organizational climate has been done by Gilbert and Levinson (1957); their research, and related work, was done in mental hospitals. A scale was developed to characterize ideology about mental illness (the Custodial Mental Illness Scale, or CMI). The structure of the instrument is quite similar to that of the F scale with most of the items stated in one direction. The items are intended to express either a custodial or a humanistic orientation toward the nature and treatment of mental illness. Conceptually, the custodial orientation or set of beliefs was regarded as congruent with authoritarian personality dispositions.

Using male aides in a state mental hospital as respondents, Pine and Levinson did a clinical evaluation of the CMI (reported in Greenblatt, Levinson, and Williams, 1957). Responses to interviews and projective materials, in addition to the CMI items, were analyzed for five high and five low scorers. They found a close correspondence among custodial beliefs, authoritarianism, and the CMI responses. According to the authors, high scorers tended to idealize their parents, to repress hostility toward family members, and to express distaste for introspection. They also tended to regard the mental patient as troublesome, to espouse strict discipline in dealing with mental patients, and to show a "non-psychological" orientation to mental illness.

With the CMI measure validated in a rough way, Gilbert and Levinson (1957) investigated the interaction of institutional policy, ideology, and personality in three mental hospitals. The three areas were expected to show a certain amount of correspondence. Four positions in the hospitals (doctor, nurse, student nurse, and aide) were ranked by the investigators on the degree of custodialism expected. The three hospitals were also ranked, based on knowledge about their general atmosphere. The two sets of ranks were then put together to yield 12 "status units." The authors treated the overall ranking as reflecting the "policy requirements" of the positions in the hospitals using it as a measure of institutional policy independent of the particular individuals occupying the positions. For the 12 groups, a high relationship was found between the organizational measure and the average CMI scores. An almost identical relationship was obtained between the former and the average F scale scores of the groups. According to the authors, the F scale provided a measure of the modal personality in the groups. Even though individual scores on the scales showed only a very moderate correlation with the 12 "policy" ranks, a higher relationship appeared between the variation of CMI and F scale scores within status units; that is, within the 12 units, a greater range of CMI scores related to a greater range of F scale scores. What the authors suggested here was a "congruence between the policy requirements of a system and the modal personality of its members . . . facilitated through recruitment, selective turnover, and possible personality changes" (Greenblatt and others, 1957, p. 32). Apparently, authoritarianism was the prior variable for individuals, with the orientation toward mental illness developing subsequently, especially in interaction with the organization. To a greater or lesser extent, the organization demanded, through its policies and climate, an orientation fitting in with its practices.

Carstairs and Heron (in Greenblatt and others, 1957) did a similar study in an English hospital. They administered both the CMI and F scales to eight different groups, including doctors, tradesmen, and student nurses. For the whole sample there was a low to moderate relationship between scores on the two scales. Group means, however, did not repeat the same high correspondence found by Gilbert and Levinson. The authors remarked that the CMI averages related closely to the educational level of the group; F scale scores and educational level showed less correspondence.

Gilbert and Levinson (in Greenblatt and others, 1957) also studied the job performance of aides. A role inventory ("Custodial Role Performance" or CRP) was used by nursing supervisors to rank the aides (e.g., how the aide persuades patients to follow routines). In a female-aide sample, CRP and CMI scores related highly, as did the CRP and F scale scores. However, the correlations were nonsignificant for a sample of male aides. The factors responsible for this difference are not clear. Toobert, Scott, and Lewis (1962) found in a large mental hospital certain ward management practices (such as privilege cards for patients, work detail, etc.) associated with low custodialism and low authoritarianism.

Using patients as respondents, a subsequent study attempting to interrelate personality, role, and social structure (Levinson and Gallagher, 1964) compared F, CMI and factor scores derived from items dealing with patienthood in a mental hospital. F scale scores and CMI related highly (r=.75) and showed similar patterns of correlation with the factor scores. The highest three correlations (.75, .64, .58) were with factors and "fusion-factors" (scales constructed with items loading highly on two factors) labeled "preference for benign autocracy and conventional facade," "optimistic reliance on external supports and controls," and "emphasis on strict control by self and by milieu," respectively. The authors conceptualized authoritarianism as the psychodynamic basis for much of the differential response to patienthood, though they included social class as an important determinant. With regard to the latter, for example, their factor "preference for benign autocracy and conventional facade" related to social class (r=.47) as well as to F. Most of the relationship between social class and the factor was accounted for in terms of the F scale, as shown also by a correlation of .13 (down from .47) between the factor and social class scores with F held constant. Social class could not account for the entire relationship. Potential response bias was contained within the factor and "fusion-factors" related to F and CMI which had all items keyed in the "agree" direction.

Work on authoritarianism involving the ties between individuals and groups has provided an acid test of the relevance of this personality syndrome for the social world. In a real sense studies of social behavior question whether or not authoritarianism makes a difference in society and the social order. Previously discussed studies yield implications of social consequences, but most of the studies remain detached from actual behaviors, even though they may be of considerable theoretical interest. The broad impact of authoritarianism on social life has not been systematically investigated, but the studies cited have begun the task.

Studies of small groups have implied some congruence between authoritarian dispositions and behavior in groups. Particularly, in the lack of sensitivity toward and distrust of others (where the situation permits) by authoritarian persons, the findings seem most clear. Researchers have also demonstrated certain predictable reactions to authority. Apparently authoritarianism (difficulties of method aside) is not inevitably expressed in certain forms of behavior, nor does membership in a particular group necessarily increase authoritarian dispositions. Situation and the social structure in which authoritarianism (or the lack of it) is embedded exercise constraints on behavior. Particularly, the expression of personality dispositions in leader or member roles may be modified by the situation in which group processes take place. Factors affecting the style of leadership or of followership in a group may override, or accentuate, or otherwise modify personality dispositions and thereby change the consequences of style (for some related discussion on this point, see Fleischman, Harris, and Burtt, 1955; Chapter 7 in Likert, 1961). Different demands made upon leaders by group members, organizational requirements, and the nature of the group task make impossible simple definitions of the relationships of authoritarianism and leadership.

Recognition of the complications makes the complex organization a potentially fruitful research site. On one hand, authoritarian dispositions can be treated as a factor mediating effects of situational, role, and structural variables on performance and attitudes. On the other hand, researchers may study organizational effects on personality itself (as in the study by Siegel and Siegel, 1957). The discussion by Levinson (1959) on role, personality, and social structure explicitly outlines these possibilities. One set of problems involves the characteristics of organizations and groups as they affect the selection of occupants for various positions. Another set concerns changes in personality and beliefs resulting from role occupancy (in the manner of the study by Lieberman, 1956). For example, although hospitals reputedly are organized along autocratic lines with emphasis placed on power and status differences by physicians (Seeman and Evans, 1961), it cannot be taken for granted that highly authoritarian personalities are selected or developed there.

Conclusion

Although difficult to summarize, the many varied findings discussed in this review can be organized into a framework of causal implications. That research results constantly raise new problems and side issues is undeniable. Yet, our knowledge of authoritarianism has moved toward greater maturity and differentiation.

First, some hypotheses contain, implicitly or explicitly, factors antecedent to the personality disposition or variables contributing to the development of authoritarianism. Relatively few of the studies cited above fall into this category, but they are an important group for a social psychological view. Included here are studies attempting to specify the social conditions which contribute to authoritarianism. For example, Lipset's discussion of the circumstances surrounding the lower socioeconomic classes would fall here. So also do the studies that take a particular social experience, such as prison or military service or some type of living group, as a causal factor in producing authoritarian dispositions. Some of the conditions are temporary or situational; others are permanent aspects of the individual's life. What is common in these conceptualizations is a restriction of social life and an exposure to a social system which embodies norms and structures corresponding to authoritarian beliefs in the individual.

As a second general category, various formulations focus on the correlates of authoritarianism, the related variables. Typically, investigators treat the occurrence of some belief or feeling as having a probability covarying with the authoritarianism of the subject. Also, researchers usually regard the subject as having a fixed amount of authoritarianism which makes it more likely that he will embrace certain political, ethnic, or religious beliefs. If one thinks of the belief systems of individuals at a certain point in time, the various linkages can be caught. For example, studies have identified prejudice toward a particular minority group as a correlate of authoritarianism. Alienation would be another example and perhaps a better one, since it is not clear whether alienation or authoritarianism should be considered as antecedent. In fact, McDill found each of these variables related to ethnocentrism when the other was controlled (McDill, 1961).

Most investigators, not satisfied to think of various correlates of authoritarianism, seek a causal sequence. Most studies we have discussed treated variables as consequences of authoritarianism that is a prior characteristic in a causal chain, having developed before particular content beliefs. Most investigators would probably maintain that the existence of authoritarianism alters the probability of subscribing to a relevant belief and add "other things being equal." The treatment of cause and effect, however, is usually only conceptual; data to establish the sequence are not (and, perhaps, cannot be) collected. For example, the finding that punitive attitudes toward international relationships are more characteristic of authoritarian respondents (Mac-

CONCLUSION

Kinnon and Centers, 1956b), or distrust of others in social relationships (Deutsch, 1960), provides evidence consistent with, but not definitive of, a causal interpretation. In the realm of group behavior authoritarianism is regarded as a factor having consequences for the satisfactions and performance of the members. Finally, authoritarianism is taken as the cause of differences in response to influence attempts (Katz and others, 1957).

As a further category, there are studies which attempt to specify conditions modifying the consequences of authoritarianism. An example would be Vroom's (1960) use of participation in an organizational setting or the finding that expressions of aggression vary with the status of the person who is the object of these expressions (Roberts and Jessor, 1958). The treatment of interactions among personality, beliefs, and organizational requirements by Gilbert and Levinson (1957) would fit here. This type of conceptualization places authoritarianism in the context of other classes of variables and explores changes in relationships as conditions vary.

As a final type of research, there are studies which attempt to establish alternative explanations to authoritarianism. On one hand, there are reformulations. Dogmatism, as developed by Rokeach and his coworkers, is an extension and reinterpretation of the work reported in *The Authoritarian Personality;* it tries to account for the same phenomena in the same general way but with modifications. The approach of Stewart and Hoult (1959) substitutes role-taking ability as the core problem and cause of authoritarianism. Alternatively, the matter of response bias in general, and acquiescence in particular, has received a great deal of attention. Response bias represents a different explanation. At the simplest level, acquiescence may be regarded as an uncontrolled intrusion into attempts at measuring authoritarianism, thereby rendering doubtful any findings. At another level, acquiescence itself can be regarded as a personality variable that has relationships to other variables. Although acquiescence may in actuality be related to authoritarianism, at this point it may be regarded as an explanation outside the realm of what the available measures of authoritarianism purport to measure.

In all these areas and ways in which authoritarianism has been investigated, uncertainties regarding findings exist. Any particular study can be questioned on various grounds, although the problem of acquiescence appears to be the most endemic shortcoming. Despite the many doubts, we think that authoritarianism is a significant phenomenon and one worthy of further attention by social science investigators. Over the whole range of studies the various alternative explanations that are possible to explain specific relationships will by no means account for all the findings. It is true that the measures of authoritarianism used relate "most systematically with other paper-and-pencil measures" (Titus and Hollander, 1957, p. 62), but it is also true that other, less questionable, relationships have been established.

We suffer from the apparent ease with which authoritarian behavior can be identified in real-life examples, especially in the pejorative use of the concept to label what appears as an unyielding, paranoid reaction to the social world. Examples of this are easily found in letters written to the editors of urban newspapers. Our confidence in a diagnosis of authoritarianism is not matched by our skill in objective measurement. Most items used to tap authoritarianism are manifest reflections of concepts close to the behaviors described. Between these low-level concepts and the abstract theory of authoritarianism, there is an enormous gap with only occasional glimpses of social and situational concepts that are connected with both abstract and concrete terminals.

CONCLUSION

The conception and execution of research in this area has suffered from the fact that authoritarianism, as it is currently formulated, is a relatively poor explanatory variable. It suggests so many connotations which have been inadequately verified. As specified in *The Authoritarian Personality*, the various components, such as rigidity and stereotypy, have not stood up as a coherent and unified set of dispositions (see, for example, the factor analysis reported by Camilleri, 1959). In fact, the concept has so many different aspects that investigators lack a common core of established meaning, and often assume connections among various dispositions that have never been examined satisfactorily. If one assumes, for instance, that the authoritarian person is more rigid in every aspect of psychological functioning and then draws some conclusions about a relationship to some belief, how do the results of research on the latter relationship bear on the nature of authoritarianism, particularly if the results obtained are negative? A related problem is the leap sometimes made from a characteristic, such as concern with power, to the whole cluster of authoritarian traits. On one hand, concern with power may not actually be related to, say, general hostility; on the other hand, indicators of concern with power, including paper-and-pencil tests, are not necessarily related to underlying dispositions. Titus and Hollander (1957, p. 62) noted an "inclination to impute a correspondence between ideology, personality, and institutional form so as to view them as having a congruence of 'authoritarian' identity."

Authoritarianism may best be viewed as a middle-level construct, one providing a coherent setting for a variety of dispositional concepts. The several aspects of authoritarianism were held by the authors of the original volume to be loosely cohering subparts of a syndrome; although a person may exhibit several of these aspects, the prototype of the authoritarian may be indeed rare. A conceptual model that holds these subparts to be more or less independently variable suggests that research efforts to date are misleading. A multivariate construct is conceptually attainable, but difficult for the researcher. The transition from construct to working definition, which, of course, cannot be avoided, produces unmanageable complications that can only be handled analytically and in turn. Beyond the most general level, the dynamics of authoritarianism as it relates to any psychological variable will be doubtful and obscure, because it is excessively speculative. This problem is compounded from a psychometric point of view when we recall that the "authoritarian" subjects studied in research are closer to the middle of the scale than to the high authoritarian end, leaving great latitude for a wide variety of response patterns in attaining similar outcomes.

No single social theory now encompasses the major findings on authoritarianism, nor has a comprehensive set of hypotheses ever been tested and revised. Nevertheless, we can outline the authoritarian from the collection of loosely associated results, although such an outline is overly simplified and can be deceptive.

Some ways of looking at authoritarianism or identifying the authoritarian probably are not fruitful. The search for specific belief items or specific behavioral responses likely will add little to our understanding of the phenomenon. Similarly, the authoritarian will not likely be identified through particular beliefs or behaviors because situational constraints, social roles, and stylized facades easily may disguise underlying functioning.

The most useful way to define authoritarianism appears to be in terms of a cognitive style—closed-minded cognitive functioning. The genuine authoritarian lacks ability to deal with novel cognitive material, seeks rapid closure when exposed to new situations, and ultimately depends heavily on external authority for support of his belief system. To be sure, the style is mediated and maintained through a set of beliefs and through patterns of behavior which themselves are subject to social reality. The particular beliefs and behaviors vary from person to person, but the style of cognition is relatively permanent. To identify the closed-minded person, an observer would need to see a range of responses, especially reactions to situations involving issues of central concern to the subject.

Certain domains of belief often serve as foci for the closed-minded style. First, certain areas of personal functioning are sensitive to powerful cultural demands that frequently elicit anxious reactions and authoritative attempts at control. Sex and aggression represent such areas in American culture. Cognitive style should be more manifest in responses to such content areas, provided that situational constraints and stylized roles can be ruled out. Second, there are institutional arenas in which the authoritarian person may more easily channel his interests. Politics is one such potential arena, where extremist groups have a cultural legitimacy. An authoritarian interested in politics is more likely to prefer conservative ideology. Another possible focus is on the nation as an idealized personification. Adherence to hostile beliefs about the relationship to other nations can be mediated by, and given a certain respectability through, nationalistic identity and patriotism. Third, the authoritarian can find convenient channels in religion, especially in fundamentalist sects or institutionalized religious authority. The appeal seems to lie in orthodoxy and sharp rejection of nonbelievers. Finally, ethnocentrism, social distance, and intolerance provide a channel for the authoritarian. A tradition of ethnic and racial hatred has been a more or less permanent feature of our society with apologists and a ready social organization. In all of these areas, the particular direction and content of beliefs is less important or less symptomatic than their function in externalization.

Because social behavior occurs in continuous transaction with an active environment, direct expression of authoritarianism may be tempered by powerful social forces. For example, what appears as bland behavior may in fact be the result of underlying distrust and fear subjected to a complex set of conflicting pressures created by social norms and the demands of authority. Also, authoritarian behavior should be distinguished from lack of sophistication or situationally-determined social conformity. Over a range of situations and events, however, the behavior of the authoritarian should reflect a picture of active distrust, submission to personally relevant authority, and hostility toward "safe" scapegoats. Evidence also points to narrow role conception and constricted role performance as a concomitant of authoritarianism. Under conditions of stress these patterns should occur more readily, particularly patterns of response serving the perceived requirements of power and authority.

Authoritarianism is not a social classification, yet those exposed to impoverished and constricted social context are more likely to develop authoritarian tendencies. Excessive emphasis on the correctness and legitimacy of authority and demands for adherence to a power structure must be counted among the social origins (see the discussion by Fromm, 1947, on authoritarian conscience and ethics).

It is most difficult to assess the role of authoritarianism in a broad social context. Research has not clearly shown to what extent "paranoid" social groups are based on an appeal to authoritarian persons, how susceptible authoritarians are to active participation in extremist movements of any kind, what effects such groups have on established social forms

CONCLUSION

and institutions, what is the epidemiology of authoritarianism, what modifications of the style are likely under certain social conditions. These questions about the social effects of authoritarianism anticipated in the original studies have yet to be investigated. A review of the field written ten years hence will hopefully provide some of the answers.

References

ABRAMS, L.
Aggressive behavior in the authoritarian. Ph.D. dissertation, University of Texas, 1965.

ADAMS, H. E., AND VIDULICH, R. N.
Dogmatism and belief congruence in paired-associate learning. *Psychological Reports,* 10: 91-94 (1962).

ADAMS, P., SCHWAB, J., AND APONTE, J.
Authoritarian parents and disturbed children. *American Journal of Psychiatry,* 121: 1162-67 (1965).

ADORNO, T. W., FRENKEL-BRUNSWIK, ELSE, LEVINSON, D. J., AND SANFORD, R. N.
The Authoritarian Personality. New York: Harper, 1950.

ALLPORT, G. W.
The Nature of Prejudice. Cambridge, Mass.: Addison-Wesley, 1954.

ANDERSON, R. C.
Learning in discussions. *Harvard Educational Review,* 29: 201-15 (1959).

ASCH, S. E.
Social Psychology. Englewood Cliffs, N.J.: Prentice-Hall, 1952.

AUMACK, L.
The effects of imprisonment upon authoritarian attitudes. *American Psychologist,* 10: 342 abstract (1955).

BARKER, E. N.
Authoritarianism of the political right, center, and left. *Journal of Social Issues,* 19: 63-74 (1963).

REFERENCES

Bass, B. M.

Authoritarianism or acquiescence? *Journal of Abnormal and Social Psychology*, 51, 616-23 (1955).

—————.

Leadership, Psychology, and Organizational Behavior. New York: Harper, 1960.

Bass, B. M., McGehee, C. R., Hawkins, W. C., Young, P. C., and Gebel, A. S.

Personality variables related to leaderless group discussion. *Journal of Abnormal and Social Psychology*, 48: 120-28 (1953).

Bendix, R., and Lipset, S. M. (Eds.).

Class, Status, and Power. Glencoe, Ill.: Free Press, 1953.

Bennis, W. G.

Leadership theory and administrative behavior: the problem of authority. *Administrative Science Quarterly*, 4: 259-301 (1959).

Berg, I. A., and Bass, B. (Eds.).

Conformity and Deviation. New York: Harper, 1961.

Berg, K.

Ethnic attitudes and agreement with a Negro person. *Journal of Personality and Social Psychology*, 4: 215-20 (1966).

Berkowitz, L.

Judgmental processes in personality functioning. *Psychological Review*, 67: 130-42 (1960).

Berkowitz, L., and Lundy, R. M.

Personality characteristics related to susceptibility to influence by peers or authority figures. *Journal of Personality*, 25: 306-16 (1957).

Berkowitz, N. H., and Wolkon, G.

A forced-choice form of the F scale—free of acquiescent response set. *Sociometry*, 27: 54-65 (1964).

Bettelheim, B., and Janowitz, M.

The Dynamics of Prejudice. New York: Harper, 1950.

Blalock, H. M., Jr.

Evaluating the relative importance of variables. *American Sociological Review*, 26: 866-74 (1961).

REFERENCES

BROWN, D. R., AND BRSTRYN, DENISE.
College environment, personality and social ideology of three ethnic groups. *Journal of Social Psychology,* 44: 279-88 (1956).

BROWN, R. W.
A determinant of the relationship between rigidity and authoritarianism. *Journal of Abnormal and Social Psychology,* 48: 469-76 (1953).

BYRNE, D.
Parental antecedents of authoritarianism. *Journal of Personality and Social Psychology,* 1: 369-73 (1965).

BYRNE, D., BLAYLOCK, B., AND GOLDBERG, J.
Dogmatism and defense mechanisms. *Psychological Reports,* 18: 739-42 (1966).

CAMILLERI, S. F.
A factor analysis of the F scale. *Social Forces,* 37:316-23 (1959).

CAMPBELL, A., CONVERSE, P. E., MILLER, W. E., AND STOKES, D. E.
The American Voter. New York: Wiley, 1960.

CAMPBELL, A., GURIN, G., AND MILLER, W. E.
Sense of political efficacy and political participation. In H. Eulau and others, *Political Behavior.* Glencoe, Ill.: Free Press, 1956.

CAMPBELL, D. T., AND MCCANDLESS, B. R.
Ethnocentrism, xenophobia, and personality. *Human Relations,* 4: 186-92 (1951).

CAMPBELL, D. T., AND MCCORMACK, THELMA H.
Military experience and attitudes toward authority. *American Journal of Sociology,* 62: 482-90 (1957).

CANNING, R. R., AND BAKER, J. M.
Effect of the group on authoritarian and non-authoritarian persons. *American Journal of Sociology,* 64: 579-81 (1959).

CAREY, GLORIA L., ROGOW, A. A., AND FARRELL, CALISTA.
The relationship between the F scale and aphorism usage and agreement. *Journal of Psychology,* 43: 163-67 (1957).

CARSTAIRS, G. M., AND HERON, A.
The social environment of mental hospital patients: a measure of staff attitudes. In M. Greenblatt and others (Eds.), *The Pa-*

REFERENCES

tient and the Mental Hospital. Glencoe, Ill.: Free Press, 1957.

CENTERS, R., AND HOROWITZ, M.
Social character and conformity: a difference in susceptibility to social influence. *Journal of Social Psychology,* 60: 343-49 (1963).

CHAPMAN, L. J., AND BOCK, R. D.
Components of variance due to acquiescence and content in the F-scale measure of authoritarianism. *Psychological Bulletin,* 55: 328-33 (1958).

CHAPMAN, L. J., AND CAMPBELL, D. T.
Response set in the F scale. *Journal of Abnormal and Social Psychology,* 54: 129-32 (1957).

—————.
The effect of acquiescence response set upon relationships among F scale, ethnocentrism, and intelligence. *Sociometry,* 22: 153-61 (1959).

CHRISTIANSEN, B.
Attitudes Toward Foreign Affairs as a Function of Personality. Oslo: Oslo University Press, 1959.

CHRISTIE, R.
Authoritarianism re-examined. In R. Christie and M. Jahoda (Eds.), *Studies in the Scope and Method of "The Authoritarian Personality."* Glencoe, Ill.: Free Press, 1954.

CHRISTIE, R., AND COOK, P.
A guide to published literature relating to the authoritarian personality through 1956. *Journal of Psychology,* 45: 171-99 (1958).

CHRISTIE, R., AND GARCIA, J.
Subcultural variation in the authoritarian personality. *Journal of Abnormal and Social Psychology,* 46: 457-69 (1951).

CHRISTIE, R., HAVEL, J., AND SEIDENBERG, B.
Is the F scale irreversible? *Journal of Abnormal and Social Psychology,* 56: 143-59 (1958).

CHRISTIE, R., AND JAHODA, MARIE (EDS.).
Studies in the Scope and Method of "The Authoritarian Personality." Glencoe, Ill.: Free Press, 1954.

140

REFERENCES

COHN, T. S.
The relation of the F scale to a response to answer positively. *American Psychologist*, 8: 335 abstract (1953).

COHN, T., AND CARSCH, H.
Administration of the F scale to a sample of Germans. *Journal of Abnormal and Social Psychology*, 49: 471 (1954).

COUCH, A., AND KENISTON, K.
Yeasayers and naysayers: agreeing response set as a personality variable. *Journal of Abnormal and Social Psychology*, 60: 151-74 (1960).

COWEN, E. L., LANDES, J., AND SCHAET, D.
The effects of mild frustration on the expression of prejudiced attitudes. *Journal of Abnormal and Social Psychology*, 58: 33-37 (1959).

CROCKETT, W. H., AND MEIDINGER, T.
Authoritarianism and interpersonal perception. *Journal of Abnormal and Social Psychology*, 53: 378-80 (1956).

CRONBACH, L. J.
Response sets and test validity. *Educational and Psychological Measurement*, 6: 475-94 (1946).

————.
Processes affecting scores on "understanding of others" and "assumed similarity." *Psychological Bulletin*, 52: 177-93 (1955).

CRUTCHFIELD, R. S.
Conformity and character. *American Psychologist*, 10: 191-98 (1955).

CUMMING, ELAINE, AND HENRY, W. E.
Growing Old. New York: Basic Books, 1961.

DAVIDS, A.
Generality and consistency of relations between the alienation syndrome and cognitive processes. *Journal of Abnormal and Social Psychology*, 51: 61-67 (1955).

————.
The influence of ego-involvement on relations between authoritarianism and intolerance of ambiguity. *Journal of Consulting Psychology*, 20: 179-84 (1956).

REFERENCES

DEAN, D. G.

Alienation: its meaning and measurement. *American Sociological Review*, 26: 753-58 (1961).

DEUTSCH, M.

Trust, trustworthiness, and the F scale. *Journal of Abnormal and Social Psychology*, 61: 138-41 (1960).

EPSTEIN, R.

Aggression toward outgroups as a function of authoritarianism and imitation of aggressive models. *Journal of Personality and Social Psychology*, 3: 574-79 (1966).

EYSENCK, H.

Response set, authoritarianism, and personality questionnaires. *British Journal of Social and Clinical Psychology*, 1: 20-24 (1962).

FILLENBAUM, S., AND JACKMAN, A.

Dogmatism and anxiety in relation to problem solving: an extension of Rokeach's results. *Journal of Abnormal and Social Psychology*, 63: 212-14 (1961).

FLEISHMAN, E. A., HARRIS, E. F., AND BURTT, H. E.

Leadership and supervision in industry. *Ohio State Business Education Research Monographs*, No. 33, 1955.

FOSTER, R. J., AND GRIGG, A. E.

Acquiescent response set as a measure of acquiescence: further evidence. *Journal of Abnormal and Social Psychology*, 67: 304-306 (1963).

FREEDMAN, M., WEBSTER, H., AND SANFORD, N.

A study of authoritarianism and psychopathology. *Journal of Psychology*, 41: 315-22 (1956).

FRENCH, E.

Interrelation among some measures of rigidity under stress and non-stress conditions. *Journal of Abnormal and Social Psychology*, 51: 114-18 (1955).

FRENKEL-BRUNSWIK, ELSE.

Further explorations by a contributor to "The Authoritarian Personality." In R. Christie and M. Jahoda (Eds.), *Studies in the Scope and Method of "The Authoritarian Personality."* Glencoe, Ill.: Free Press, 1954.

REFERENCES

————.
Intolerance of ambiguity as an emotional and perceptual variable. *Journal of Personality*, 18: 108-43 (1949).

FROMM, E.
Man for Himself. New York: Rinehart, 1947.

FRUCHTER, B., ROKEACH, M., AND NOVAK, E. G.
A factorial study of dogmatism, opinionation and related scales. *Psychological Reports*, 4: 19-22 (1958).

GAGE, N. L., AND CHATTERGEE, B. B.
The psychological meaning of acquiescence set: further evidence. *Journal of Abnormal and Social Psychology*, 60: 280-83 (1960).

GAGE, N. L., LEAVITT, G. S., AND STONE, G. C.
The psychological meaning of acquiescent set. *Journal of Abnormal and Social Psychology*, 55: 98-103 (1957).

GIBB, C. A.
Leadership. In G. Lindzey (Ed.), *Handbook of Social Psychology.* Cambridge, Mass.: Addison-Wesley, 1954.

GILBERT, D. C., AND LEVINSON, D. J.
Ideology, personality, and institutional policy in the mental hospital. *Journal of Abnormal and Social Psychology*, 53: 263-71 (1956).

————.
Role performance, ideology and personality in mental hospital aides. In M. Greenblatt and others (Eds.), *The Patient and the Mental Hospital.* Glencoe, Ill.: Free Press, 1957.

GLADSTONE, A. I., AND TAYLOR, M. A.
Threat-related attitudes and reactions to communications about international events. *Journal of Conflict Resolution*, 2: 17-28 (1958).

GREENBERG, H., GUERINO, R., LASHEN, M., MEYER, D., AND PISKOWSKI, D.
Order of birth as a determinant of personality and attitudinal characteristics. *Journal of Social Psychology*, 60: 221-30 (1963).

GREENBLATT, M., LEVINSON, D. J., AND WILLIAMS, R. H. (EDS.).
The Patient and the Mental Hospital. Glencoe, Ill.: Free Press, 1957.

REFERENCES

GREENSTEIN, F.

Personality and political socialization: the theories of authoritarian and democratic character. *Annals of the American Academy of Political and Social Science*, 361: 81-95 (1965).

GREGORY, W. E.

The orthodoxy of the authoritarian personality. *Journal of Social Psychology*, 45: 217-32 (1957).

GRUSKY, O.

Authoritarianism and effective indoctrination: a case study. *Administrative Science Quarterly*, 7: 79-95 (1962).

GURIN, G., VEROFF, J., AND FELD, SHEILA.

Americans View Their Mental Health. New York: Basic Books, 1960.

HARDING, J., KUTNER, B., PROSHANSKY, H., AND CHEIN, I.

Prejudice and ethnic relations. In G. Lindzey (Ed.), *Handbook of Social Psychology*. Cambridge, Mass.: Addison-Wesley, 1954.

HARNED, LOUISE.

Authoritarian attitudes and party activity. *Public Opinion Quarterly*, 25: 393-99 (1961).

HART, I.

Maternal child-rearing practices and authoritarian ideology. *Journal of Abnormal and Social Psychology*, 55: 232-37 (1957).

HARVEY, O. J.

Authoritarianism and conceptual functioning in varied conditions. *Journal of Personality*, 31: 462-70 (1963).

————.

Personality factors in resolution of conceptual incongruities. *Sociometry*, 25: 336-52 (1962).

HARVEY, O. J., AND BEVERLY, G.

Some personality correlates of concept change through role playing. *Journal of Abnormal and Social Psychology*, 63: 125-30 (1961).

HARVEY, O. J., AND CALDWELL, D.

Assimilation and contrast phenomena in response to environmental variation. *Journal of Personality*, 27: 125-35 (1959).

144

REFERENCES

HAYTHORN, W., COUCH, A., HAEFNER, D., LANGHAM, P., AND CARTER, L.
The behavior of authoritarian and equalitarian personalities in small groups. *Human Relations,* 9: 57-74 (1956a).
──────.
The effects of varying combinations of authoritarian and equalitarian leaders and followers. *Journal of Abnormal and Social Psychology,* 53: 210-19 (1956b).
HESLIN, R.
Predicting group task effectiveness from member characteristics. *Psychological Bulletin,* 62: 248-56 (1964).
HITES, R. W., AND KELLOG, E. P.
The F and Social Maturity Scales in relation to racial attitudes in a deep south sample. *Journal of Social Psychology,* 62: 189-95 (1964).
HOFFER, E.
The True Believer. New York: Mentor Books, 1958.
HOFFMAN, M.
Conformity as a defense mechanism and a form of resistance to genuine group influence. *Journal of Personality,* 25: 412-24 (1957).
HOFSTADTER, R.
The Paranoid Style in American Politics. New York: Knopf, 1965.
HOVLAND, C. I., JANIS, I. L., AND KELLEY, H. H.
Communication and Persuasion. New Haven, Conn.: Yale University Press, 1953.
HYMAN, H. H.
Survey Design and Analysis. Glencoe, Ill.: Free Press, 1955.
HYMAN, H. H., AND SHEATSLEY, P. B.
"The Authoritarian Personality": a methodological critique. In R. Christie and M. Jahoda (Eds.), *Studies in the Scope and Method of "The Authoritarian Personality."* Glencoe, Ill.: Free Press, 1954.
JACKSON, D. N.
Cognitive energy level, acquiescence and authoritarianism. *Journal of Social Psychology,* 49: 65-69 (1959).

REFERENCES

JACKSON, D. N., AND MESSICK, S. J.
A note on "ethnocentrism" and acquiescent response sets. *Journal of Abnormal and Social Psychology*, 54: 132-34 (1957).

JACKSON, D. N., MESSICK, S. J., AND SOLLEY, C. M.
How "rigid" is the "authoritarian"? *Journal of Abnormal and Social Psychology*, 54: 137-40 (1957).

JANOWITZ, M., AND MARVICK, D.
Authoritarianism and political behavior. *Public Opinion Quarterly*, 17: 185-201 (1953).

JENSEN, A. R.
Authoritarian attitudes and personality maladjustment. *Journal of Abnormal and Social Psychology*, 54: 303-11 (1957).

JOHNSON, R. C., JOHNSON, CAROL, AND MARTIN, LEA.
Authoritarianism, occupation and sex role differentiation of children. *Child Development*, 32: 271-76 (1961).

JONES, E. E.
Authoritarianism as a determinant of first-impression formation. *Journal of Personality*, 23: 107-27 (1954).

JONES, M. B.
Note on authoritarian confinement and scholastic aptitude. *Psychological Reports*, 2: 461-64 (1956).

KAHN, R., WOLFE, D., QUINN, R., SNOEK, J., AND ROSENTHAL, R.
Organizational Stress: Studies in Role Conflict and Ambiguity. New York: Wiley, 1964.

KATES, S. L., AND DIAB, L. N.
Authoritarian ideology and attitudes on parent-child relationships. *Journal of Abnormal and Social Psychology*, 51: 13-16 (1955).

KATZ, D., McCLINTOCK, C., AND SARNOFF, I.
The measurement of ego defense as related to attitude change. *Journal of Personality*, 25: 465-74 (1957).

KATZ, D., AND STOTLAND, E.
A preliminary statement to a theory of attitude structure and change. In S. Koch (Ed.), *Formulations of the Person and the Social Context.* New York: McGraw-Hill, 1959.

KATZ, I., AND BENJAMIN, L.
Effects of white authoritarianism in biracial work groups.

146

REFERENCES

Journal of Abnormal and Social Psychology, 61: 448-56 (1960).

KAUFMAN, W. C.
Status, authoritarianism, and anti-Semitism. *American Journal of Sociology,* 62: 379-82 (1957).

KELMAN, H. C., AND BARCLAY, JANET.
The F scale as a measure of breadth of perspective. *Journal of Abnormal and Social Psychology,* 67: 608-15 (1963).

KENNY, D. T., AND GINSBERG, ROSE.
Authoritarian submission attitudes, intolerance of ambiguity and aggression. *Canadian Journal of Psychology,* 12: 121-26 (1958).

KERLINGER, F., AND ROKEACH, M.
The factorial nature of the F and D scales. *Journal of Personality and Social Psychology,* 4: 391-99 (1966).

KNOPFELMACHER, F., AND ARMSTRONG, D.
Authoritarianism, ethnocentrism and religious denomination. *American Catholic Sociological Review,* 24: 99-114 (1963).

KOGAN, N.
Authoritarianism and repression. *Journal of Abnormal and Social Psychology,* 53: 34-37 (1956).

KRUG, R.
An analysis of the F scale: I. Item factor analysis. *Journal of Social Psychology,* 53: 285-91 (1961).

KUTNER, B., AND GORDON, N.
Cognitive functioning and prejudice: a nine-year follow-up study. *Sociometry,* 27: 66-74 (1964).

LANE, R. E.
Political personality and electoral choice. *American Political Science Review,* 49: 173-90 (1955).

LASKY, J.
Effect of prestige suggestion and peer standards on California F scale scores. *Psychological Reports,* 11: 187-91 (1962).

LEAVITT, H. J., HAX, H., AND ROCHE, J. H.
"Authoritarianism" and agreement with things authoritative. *Journal of Psychology,* 40: 215-21 (1955).

LEVENTHAL, H., JACOBS, R., AND KUDIRKA, N.
Authoritarianism, ideology, and political candidate choice.

REFERENCES

Journal of Abnormal and Social Psychology, 69: 539-49 (1964).

LEVINSON, D. J.
Authoritarian personality and foreign policy. *Journal of Conflict Resolution,* 1: 37-47 (1957).

————.
Role, personality and social structure in the organizational setting. *Journal of Abnormal and Social Psychology,* 58: 170-80 (1959).

LEVINSON, D. J., AND GALLAGHER, E. B.
Patienthood in the Mental Hospital. Boston: Houghton-Mifflin, 1964.

LEVINSON, D. J., AND HUFFMAN, P. E.
Traditional family ideology and its relation to personality. *Journal of Personality,* 23: 251-73 (1955).

LEVITT, E., AND ZUCKERMAN, M.
The water jar test revisited: the replication of a review. *Psychological Reports,* 5: 365-80 (1959).

LIBO, L.
Authoritarianism and attitudes toward socialized medicine among senior medical students. *Journal of Social Psychology,* 46: 133-36 (1957).

LICHTENSTEIN, E., QUINN, R. P., AND HOVER, G. L.
Dogmatism and acquiescent response set. *Journal of Abnormal and Social Psychology,* 63: 636-38 (1961).

LIEBERMAN, S.
The effects of changes in roles on the attitudes of role occupants. *Human Relations,* 9: 385-402 (1956).

LIKERT, R.
New Patterns of Management. New York: McGraw-Hill, 1961.

LINDZEY, G. (ED.).
Handbook of Social Psychology. Cambridge, Mass.: Addison-Wesley, 1954.

LIPSET, S. M.
Democracy and working class authoritarianism. *American Sociological Review,* 24: 482-501 (1959).

————.
Political Man. New York: Doubleday, 1960.

148

REFERENCES

LIPSITZ, L.

Working class authoritarianism: a re-evaluation. *American Sociological Review*, 30: 103-109 (1965).

LYLE, W. H., JR., AND LEVITT, E. E.

Punitiveness, authoritarianism, and parental discipline of grade school children. *Journal of Abnormal and Social Psychology*, 51: 42-46 (1955).

McCARTHY, J., AND JOHNSON, R. C.

Interpretation of the "City Hall Riots" as a function of general dogmatism. *Psychological Reports*, 11: 243-45 (1962).

McCLINTOCK, C.

Personality syndromes and attitude change. *Journal of Personality*, 26: 479-93 (1958).

McCLOSKY, H.

Conservatism and personality. *American Political Science Review*, 52: 27-45 (1958).

McDILL, E. L.

Anomie, authoritarianism, prejudice, and socio-economic status: an attempt at clarification. *Social Forces*, 39: 239-45 (1961).

MacKINNON, W. J., AND CENTERS, R.

Authoritarianism and internationalism. *Public Opinion Quarterly*, 20: 621-30 (1956-1957b).

————.

Authoritarianism and urban stratification. *American Journal of Sociology*, 61: 610-20 (1956a).

————.

Some aspects of opinion and personality. *Journal of Social Psychology*, 60: 339-42 (1963).

MARTIN, J. G., AND WESTIE, F. R.

The tolerant personality. *American Sociological Review*, 24: 521-28 (1959).

MASLOW, A. H.

The authoritarian character structure. *Journal of Social Psychology*, 18: 401-11 (1943).

MEDALIA, N. Z.

Authoritarianism, leader acceptance, and group cohesion. *Journal of Abnormal and Social Psychology*, 51: 207-13 (1955).

149

REFERENCES

MESSICK, S. J.

Separate set and content scores for personality and attitude scales. *Educational and Psychological Measurement*, 21: 915-23 (1961).

MESSICK, S., AND FREDERIKSEN, N.

Ability, acquiescence and authoritarianism. *Psychological Reports*, 4: 687-97 (1958).

MESSICK, S., AND JACKSON, D. N.

Authoritarianism or acquiescence in Bass's data. *Journal of Abnormal and Social Psychology*, 54: 424-27 (1957).

————.

The measurement of authoritarian attitudes. *Educational and Psychological Measurement*, 18: 241-53 (1958).

MILLER, S. M., AND RIESSMAN, F.

"Working class authoritarianism": a critique of Lipset. *British Journal of Sociology*, 12: 263-76 (1961).

MILLON, T. A.

Intolerance of ambiguity and rigidity under ego- and task-involving conditions. *Journal of Abnormal and Social Psychology*, 55: 29-33 (1957).

MISCHEL, W., AND SCHOPLER, J.

Authoritarianism and reactions to "Sputniks." *Journal of Abnormal and Social Psychology*, 59: 142-45 (1959).

MOWRY, H. W.

A measure of supervisory quality. *Journal of Applied Psychology*, 41: 405-408 (1957).

NADLER, E.

Yielding, authoritarianism, and authoritarian ideology regarding groups. *Journal of Abnormal and Social Psychology*, 58: 408-10 (1959).

NIEMS, R., AND SCODEL, A.

Authoritarianism and level of aspiration scores. *Journal of Social Psychology*, 43: 209-15 (1956).

NIYEKAWA, A. M.

Factors associated with authoritarianism in Japan. Ph.D. dissertation, New York University, 1960.

REFERENCES

PANNES, ERNESTINE D.
The relationship between self-acceptance and dogmatism in junior-senior high school students. *Journal of Educational Sociology*, 36: 419-26 (1963).

PEABODY, D.
Attitude content and agreement set in scales of authoritarianism, dogmatism, anti-Semitism and economic conservatism. *Journal of Abnormal and Social Psychology*, 63: 1-12 (1961).

—————.

Authoritarianism scales and response bias. *Psychological Bulletin*, 65: 11-23 (1966).

—————.

Models for estimating content and set components in attitude and personality scales. *Educational and Psychological Measurement*, 24: 255-69 (1964).

PETTIGREW, T. F.
Personality and sociocultural factors in intergroup attitudes: a cross-national comparison. *Journal of Conflict Resolution*, 2: 29-42 (1958a).

—————.

Social psychology and desegregation research. *American Psychologist*, 16: 105-12 (1961).

—————.

The measurement and correlates of category width as a cognitive variable. *Journal of Personality*, 26: 532-44 (1958b).

PHOTIADIS, J., AND JOHNSON, A.
Orthodoxy, church participation, and authoritarianism. *American Journal of Sociology*, 69: 244-48 (1963).

PINE, F., AND LEVINSON, D. J.
Two patterns of ideology, role conception, and personality among mental hospital aides. In M. Greenblatt, D. J. Levinson, and R. H. Williams (Eds.), *The Patient and the Mental Hospital*. Glencoe, Ill.: Free Press, 1957.

PLANT, W., TELFORD, C., AND THOMAS, J.
Some personality differences between dogmatic and nondogmatic groups. *Journal of Social Psychology*, 67: 67-75 (1965).

REFERENCES

POWELL, F.

Open- and closed-mindedness and the ability to differentiate source and message. *Journal of Abnormal and Social Psychology*, 65: 61-64 (1962).

PROTHRO, E. T.

Ethnocentrism and anti-Negro attitudes in the deep south. *Journal of Abnormal and Social Psychology*, 47: 105-108 (1952).

PROTHRO, E. T., AND MELIKIAN, L.

The California public opinion scale in an authoritarian culture. *Public Opinion Quarterly*, 17: 353-62 (1953).

QUINN, R. P.

Conformity, personality, and the extraneous third variable—acquiescence response set. Ph.D. dissertation, University of Michigan, 1963.

QUINN, R. P., AND LICHTENSTEIN, E.

Acquiescence response set in the F scale. Unpublished manuscript.

RABINOWITZ, W.

A note on the sociological perceptions of authoritarians and non-authoritarians. *Journal of Abnormal and Social Psychology*, 53: 384-86 (1956).

RESTLE, F., ANDREWS, M., AND ROKEACH, M.

Differences between open- and closed-minded subjects on learning-set and oddity problems. *Journal of Abnormal and Social Psychology*, 68: 648-54 (1964).

RHODES, A. L.

Authoritarianism and alienation: the F scale and the Srole scale as predictors of prejudice. *Sociological Quarterly*, 2: 193-202 (1961).

RHYNE, E. H.

Racial prejudice and personality scales: an alternative approach. *Social Forces*, 41: 44-53 (1962).

RICHERT, KAYE C.

Explorations into the specific behavioral determinants of authoritarians. *Psychological Reports*, 13: 950 (1963).

ROBERTS, A. H., AND JESSOR, R.

Authoritarianism, punitiveness and perceived social status.

REFERENCES

Journal of Abnormal and Social Psychology, 56: 311-14 (1958).

ROBERTS, A. H., AND ROKEACH, M.

Anomie, authoritarianism, and prejudice: a replication. *American Journal of Sociology,* 61: 355-58 (1956).

ROKEACH, M.

Authority, authoritarianism, and conformity. In I. A. Berg and B. M. Bass (Eds.), *Conformity and Deviation.* New York: Harper, 1961.

—————.

Generalized mental rigidity as a factor in ethnocentrism. *Journal of Abnormal and Social Psychology,* 43: 259-78 (1948).

—————.

The double agreement phenomenon: Three hypotheses. *Psychological Review,* 70: 304-309 (1963).

—————.

The Open and Closed Mind. New York: Basic Books, 1960.

ROKEACH, M., AND FRUCHTER, B.

A factorial study of dogmatism and related concepts. *Journal of Abnormal and Social Psychology,* 53: 356-60 (1956).

RORER, L. G.

The great response-style myth. *Psychological Bulletin,* 63: 129-56 (1965).

ROSE, A.

Prejudice, anomie, and the authoritarian personality. *Sociology and Social Research,* 50: 141-47 (1966).

ROSENBERG, M.

Misanthropy and attitudes toward international affairs. *Journal of Conflict Resolution,* 1: 340-45 (1958).

SAMELSON, F.

Agreement set and anticontent attitudes in the F scale: a reinterpretation. *Journal of Abnormal and Social Psychology,* 68: 338-42 (1964).

SANFORD, F. H.

Authoritarianism and Leadership. Philadelphia: Institute for Research in Human Relations, 1950.

SANFORD, N.

The approach of the authoritarian personality. In J. L.

REFERENCES

McCary (Ed.), *Psychology of Personality: Six Modern Approaches,* New York: Logos Press, 1956.

SARNOFF, I., AND KATZ, D.
The motivational bases of attitude change. *Journal of Abnormal and Social Psychology,* 49: 115-24 (1954).

SCHULBERG, H. C.
Authoritarianism, tendency to agree, and interpersonal perception. *Journal of Abnormal and Social Psychology,* 63: 101-108 (1961).

SCHUTZ, W. C.
What makes groups productive? *Human Relations,* 8: 429-65 (1955).

SCODEL, A., AND FREEDMAN, M. L.
Additional observations on the social perceptions of authoritarians and non-authoritarians. *Journal of Abnormal and Social Psychology,* 52: 92-95 (1956).

SCODEL, A., AND MUSSEN, P.
Social perceptions of authoritarians and non-authoritarians. *Journal of Abnormal and Social Psychology,* 48: 181-84 (1953).

SEEMAN, M.
On the meaning of alienation. *American Sociological Review,* 24: 782-91 (1959).

SEEMAN, M., AND EVANS, J.
Stratification and hospital care. *American Sociological Review,* 26: 67-79 (1961).

SHELLEY, H. P.
Response set and the California attitude scales. *Educational and Psychological Measurement,* 16: 63-67 (1956).

SHERMAN, SUSAN R.
Demand characteristics in research on attitude change. *American Psychologist,* 20: 509 abstract (1965).

SHILS, E. A.
Authoritarianism: right and left. In R. Christie and M. Jahoda (Eds.), *Studies in the Scope and Method of "The Authoritarian Personality."* Glencoe, Ill.: Free Press, 1954.

SHOBEN, E. J., JR.
The assessment of parental attitudes in relation to child adjust-

REFERENCES

ment. *Genetic Psychology Monographs,* 39: 101-48 (1949).

SIEGEL, A. E., AND SIEGEL, S.

Reference groups, membership groups, and attitude change. *Journal of Abnormal and Social Psychology,* 55: 360-64 (1957).

SIEGEL, S. M.

The relationship of hostility to authoritarianism. *Journal of Abnormal and Social Psychology,* 52: 368-72 (1956).

SIEGMAN, A. W.

A cross-cultural investigation of the relationship between ethnic prejudice, authoritarian ideology, and personality. *Journal of Abnormal and Social Psychology,* 63: 654-55 (1961).

SIMON, H. A.

Spurious correlation: a causal interpretation. *Journal of American Statistical Association,* 49: 467-79 (1954).

SIMON, W.

The quest for subjective certainty. *Journal of Social Psychology,* 66: 171-85 (1965).

SIMPSON, G. E., AND YINGER, J. M.

Racial and Cultural Minorities: An Analysis of Prejudice and Discrimination. Rev. ed. New York: Harper, 1958.

SMITH, C. U., AND PROTHRO, J. W.

Ethnic differences in the authoritarian personality. *Social Forces,* 35: 334-38 (1957).

SMITH, H. P., AND ROSEN, ELLEN W.

Some psychological correlates of world-mindedness and authoritarianism. *Journal of Personality,* 26: 170-83 (1958).

SMITH, M. B.

An analysis of two measures of "authoritarianism" among Peace Corps teachers. *Journal of Personality,* 33: 513-35 (1965).

————.

Review of "The Authoritarian Personality." *Journal of Abnormal and Social Psychology,* 45: 775-79 (1950).

————.

Review of "The Open and Closed Mind." *Science,* 132: 142-43 (1960).

SMITH, M. B., BRUNER, J. S., AND WHITE, R. W.

Opinions and Personality. New York: Wiley, 1956.

REFERENCES

SOLOMON, A.
Authoritarian attitude changes and group homogeneity. *Journal of Social Psychology*, 59: 129-35 (1963).

SROLE, L.
Social integration and certain corollaries: an exploratory study. *American Sociological Review*, 21: 709-16 (1956).

STAGNER, R.
Fascist attitudes: an exploratory study. *Journal of Social Psychology*, 7: 309-19 (1936).

STANLEY, G., AND MARTIN, J.
How sincere is the dogmatist? *Psychological Review*, 71: 331-34 (1964).

STECKLER, G. A.
Authoritarian ideology and Negro college students. *Journal of Abnormal and Social Psychology*, 54: 396-99 (1957).

STEIN, D., HARDYCK, J., AND SMITH, M. B.
Race and belief: an open and shut case. *Journal of Personality and Social Psychology*, 1: 281-89 (1965).

STEINER, I., AND JOHNSON, H.
Authoritarianism and conformity. *Sociometry*, 26: 21-34 (1963b).

—————.
Authoritarianism and "tolerance of trait inconsistency." *Journal of Abnormal and Social Psychology*, 67: 388-91 (1963a).

STEINER, I., AND VANNOY, J.
Personality correlates of two types of conformity behavior. *Journal of Personality and Social Psychology*, 4: 307-15 (1966).

STEMBER, C. H.
Education and Attitude Change. New York: Institute of Human Relations Press, 1961.

STEWART, D., AND HOULT, T.
A social-psychological theory of "The Authoritarian Personality." *American Journal of Sociology*, 65: 274-79 (1959).

STOTLAND, E., KATZ, D., AND PATCHEN, M.
The reduction of prejudice through the arousal of self-insight. *Journal of Personality*, 27: 507-31 (1959).

156

REFERENCES

STOUFFER, S. A.

Communism, Conformity, and Civil Liberties. Garden City, N.Y.: Doubleday, 1955.

SULLIVAN, P. L., AND ADELSON, J.

Ethnocentrism and misanthropy. *Journal of Abnormal and Social Psychology,* 49: 246-50 (1954).

THIBAUT, J. W., AND RIECKEN, H. W.

Authoritarianism, status, and communication of aggression. *Human Relations,* 8: 95-120 (1955).

TITUS, H. E., AND HOLLANDER, E. P.

The California F scale in psychological research: 1950-1955. *Psychological Bulletin,* 54: 47-64 (1957).

TOOBERT, S., SCOTT, F., AND LEWIS, J.

Relation of various indicators of ward management to measures of staff attitudes in a large mental hospital. *Journal of Health and Human Behavior,* 3: 185-93 (1962).

TRIANDIS, H. C.

A note on Rokeach's theory of prejudice. *Journal of Abnormal and Social Psychology,* 62: 184-86 (1961).

TRIANDIS, H. C., AND TRIANDIS, LEIGH M.

Race, social class, religion, and nationality as determinants of social distance. *Journal of Abnormal and Social Psychology,* 61: 110-18 (1960).

TRIANDIS, H., DAVIS, E., AND TAKEZAWA, S.

Some determinants of social distance among American, German, and Japanese students. *Journal of Personality and Social Psychology,* 2: 540-51 (1965).

VAUGHAN, G., AND WHITE, K.

Conformity and authoritarianism re-examined. *Journal of Personality and Social Psychology,* 3: 363-66 (1966).

VIDULICH, R. N., AND KAIMAN, I. P.

The effects of information source status and dogmatism upon conformity behavior. *Journal of Abnormal and Social Psychology,* 63: 639-42 (1961).

VROOM, V. H.

Some personality correlates of participation. *Journal of Abnormal and Social Psychology,* 59: 322-27 (1959).

REFERENCES

—————.
Some personality determinants of the effects of participation. Ph.D. dissertation, University of Michigan, 1958.

VROOM, V. H., AND MANN, F. C.
Leader authoritarianism and employee attitude. *Personnel Psychology*, 13: 125-40 (1960).

WAGMAN, M.
Attitude change and authoritarian personality. *Journal of Psychology*, 40: 3-24 (1955).

WARSHAY, L., GOLDMAN, M., AND BIDDLE, E.
Anomie and F scales as related to social characteristics. *Journal of Social Psychology*, 62: 117-23 (1964).

WEBSTER, H., SANFORD, N., AND FREEDMAN, M.
A new instrument for studying authoritarianism in personality. *Journal of Psychology*, 40: 73-84 (1955).

WEIMA, J.
Authoritarianism, religious conservatism, and sociocentric attitudes in Roman Catholic groups. *Human Relations*, 18: 231-39 (1965).

WEINER, H., AND McGINNIES, E.
Authoritarianism, conformity, and confidence in a perceptual judgment situation. *Journal of Social Psychology*, 55: 77-84 (1961).

WELLS, W. D., CHIARAVALLO, G., AND GOLDMAN, S.
Brothers under the skin: a validity test of the F scale. *Journal of Social Psychology*, 45: 35-40 (1957).

WELLS, W. D., WEINERT, G., AND RUBEL, M.
Conformity pressure and authoritarian personality. *Journal of Psychology*, 42:133-36 (1956).

WHITE, B., AND HARVEY, O. J.
Effects of personality and own stand on judgment and production of statements about a central issue. *Journal of Experimental Social Psychology*, 1: 334-47 (1965).

WHITE, J., ALTER, R., AND RARDIN, M.
Authoritarianism, dogmatism, and usage of conceptual categories. *Journal of Personality and Social Psychology*, 2: 293-95 (1965).

158

REFERENCES

WILLIAMS, C. D.
Authoritarianism and student reaction to airplane hijacking. *Journal of Social Psychology*, 60: 289-91 (1963).

WILLIAMS, E. I., JR., AND WILLIAMS, C. D.
Relationships between authoritarian attitudes of college students, estimation of parents' attitudes, and actual parental attitudes. *Journal of Social Psychology*, 61: 43-48 (1963).

WRIGHTSMAN, L. S., JR.
Authoritarianism and self-awareness. *Journal of Social Psychology*, 56: 179-85 (1962).

ZAGONA, S., AND ZURCHER, L.
Participation, interaction, and role behavior in groups selected from the extreme of the open-closed cognitive continuum. *Journal of Psychology*, 58: 255-64 (1964).

ZUCKERMAN, M., AND EISEN, BARBARA.
Relationship of acquiescence response set to authoritarianism and dependency. *Psychological Reports*, 10: 95-102 (1962).

Index

Abrams, L.: 52

Acquiescence. *See* Response bias

Adams, H., and Vidulich, R.: 49

Adams, P., Schwab, J., and Aponte, J.: 73-74

Adorno, T.: 24; Frenkel-Brunswik, E., Levinson, D., and Sanford, R., 48

Aggression, authoritarian: defined, 6; in children, 73, 75; models to lower aggression, 113

Alienation: higher among lower socioeconomic groups, 38; measure of, *see* Davids; Dean. *See also* "Alienation," 78-81

Alter, R. *See* J. White

Andrews, M. *See* Restle

Anomia: defined by Srole, 38; associated with lower socioeconomic status, 38; relation to prejudice, 89-90

Antidemocratic Scale for Children: 74-75

Anti-intraception: 6

Anxiety: 46-50

Aponte, J. *See* P. Adams

Armstrong, D. *See* Knopfelmacher

Asch, S.: 8

Attitude change: 97-102

Aumack, L.: 103-104

Authoritarian Personality, The: central thesis, 4-5; sampling procedures criticized, 31-32; no representative population, 35; important role of antidemocratic ten-

Authoritarian Personality (continued): dencies, 57. *See also* "Some Criticisms of *The Authoritarian Personality*," 7-12

Authoritarianism: subparts defined, 5-6; alternatives to, 9-11; complex nature and low content reliability, 18; rarely dependent variable, 30-31; response to anxiety, 49-50; inadequately verified, 131; measures of, *see* Berkowitz and Wolkon; M. Smith; Webster, Sanford, and Freedman

Baker, J. *See* Canning

Barclay, J. *See* Kelman

Barker, B.: 58

Barker, E.: 10

Bass, B.: content and response bias, 16; basis of forced-choice F scale by Berkowitz and Wolkon, 32, 34; McGehee, C., Hawkins, W., Young, P., and Gebel, A., 117-18

Beliefs: 55-94

Benjamin, N. *See* I. Katz

Berkeley studies: 4-7

Berkowitz, L.: 46; and Lundy, R., 111

Berkowitz, N., and Wolkon, G.: 32, 34

Bettelheim, B., and Janowitz, M.: 88

Beverly, G. *See* Harvey

Blaylock, B. *See* Byrne

Bock, R. *See* Chapman

Brown, D., and Brstryn, D.: 37

161

INDEX

Brown, R.: 43
Bruner, J. *See* M. Smith
Brstryn, D. *See* D. Brown
Byrne, D.: 76-77; Blaylock, B., and Goldberg, J., 52-53

Caldwell, D. *See* Harvey and Caldwell.
Campbell, A.—Converse, P., Miller, W., and Stokes, D.: item reversal in F scale, 17; F scale negatively related to education, 40; party affiliation unrelated to authoritarianism, 58; correlates of conservatism, 60-61, 62; —Gurin, G., and Miller, W.: 38
Campbell, D.: and McCandless, B., 85-86; and McCormack, T., 105. *See also* Chapman
Canning, R., and Baker, J.: 108-109
Carey, G., Rogow, A., and Farrell, C., 15
Carsch, H. *See* Cohn
Carstairs, G., and Heron, A.: 123
Carter, L. *See* Haythorn
Catholicism: 70, 71, 72
Centers, R.: and Horowitz, M., 109. *See also* MacKinnon
Chapman, L.: and Bock, R., 18; and Campbell, D., 16, 17
Chattergee, B. *See* Gage
Chiaravallo, G. *See* Wells
Christiansen, B.: 67-68
Christie, R.: authoritarianism of left and F scale, 10; influences other than response bias, 17; basis of forced-choice F scale by Berkowitz and Wolkon, 32, 34; F scale negatively related to education, 40; —Havel, J., and Seidenberg, B.: 25; —and Jahoda, M.: criticized *The Authoritarian Personality*, 4-5; support for content interpretation of response bias, 28-29
Cohn, T.: 14; and Carsch, H., 35-36
Conformity: 108-12
Conservatism-liberalism: F scale and measure of right, 10; related to

Conservatism-liberalism (*continued*): authoritarianism measures, 57-58; measure of, 59-60; relationship to party, 60; and paranoid style, 62-63
Conventionalism: 5
Converse, P. *See* A. Campbell
Couch, A.—and Keniston, K.: response bias, 14; item reversal in F scale, 16; response bias distinguished from authoritarianism, 25; found no association between Hysteria scale and tendency to agree, 51. *See also* Haythorn
Cowen, E., Landes, J., and Schaet, D.: 90-91
Crockett, W., and Meidinger, T.: 82
Cronbach, L: response bias, 13; invalid analyses attributed to F scale scores, 81-82
Crutchfield, R.: 108
Cultural differences: cross cultural, 35-37; subcultural effects and authoritarianism, 37-41
Cumming, E., and Henry, W.: 9
Custodial Mental Illness Scale. *See* Gilbert and Levinson

D scale. *See* Dogmatism
Davids, A.: criticized paper-and-pencil measures of intolerance of ambiguity, 43; alienation as set of related personality dispositions, 79
Davis, E. *See* Triandis
Dean, D.: 78-79
Defensiveness: 97-99
Destructiveness: 6
Deutsch, M.: high and low F scale scores and partner trustingness, 108; distrust of others in social relationships, 129
Diab, L. *See* Kates
Dogmatism: scale developed by Rokeach, 10-11; problem of response bias, 11; relation of D and F scales, 11-12; dogmatic individuals and differentiation of source and message, 110-11. *See also* "Dogmatism and Anxiety," 46-50

INDEX

E scale. *See* Ethnocentrism

Education: influence on F scale, 35; varied relationships to prejudice, 40-41

Eisen, B. *See* Zuckerman

Epstein, R.: 113

Ethnic beliefs: 84-92

Ethnocentrism: 85-86

Eysenck, H.: 18

F scale: indirect measure of prejudice, 5; reviewed by Titus and Hollander, 8-9; Kelman and Barclay interpretation, 9-10; relation to D scale, 11-12; influenced by response bias, 13-29; cross cultural use, 35-37; relation to subcultural characteristics, 37-39; relation to sophistication, 39-41; problem of itself measuring beliefs, 56; relates best to ethnic intolerance, 93-94. *See also* "Use of the F Scale: Problems and Alternatives," 29-34

Family: 72-78

Farrell, C. *See* Carey

Fascism: 5. *See also* F scale

Feld, S. *See* Gurin

Fillenbaum, S., and Jackman, A.: 49

Foster, R., and Grigg, A.: 17

Frederiksen, N. *See* Messick

Freedman, M.: Webster, H., and Sanford, N., 50-51. *See also* Scodel; Webster

French, E.: 43

Frenkel-Brunswik, E.: 75-76. *See also* Adorno

Fruchter, B.: Rokeach, M., and Novak, E., 48. *See also* Rokeach

Gage, N.—and Chattergee, B.: 23-24; —Leavitt, G., and Stone, G.: response bias, 14; positive items enhance F scale scores, 23-24

Gallagher, E. *See* Levinson

Gebel, A. *See* Bass

Gilbert, D., and Levinson, D.: Custodial Mental Illness Scale, 121; interaction of institutional policy, ideology, and personality in three

Gilbert (*continued*):
mental hospitals, 122-23, 129; job rating of aides by supervisors, 123

Ginsberg, Rose. *See* Kenny

Gladstone, A., and Taylor, M.: 67

Goldberg, J. *See* Byrne

Goldman, M. *See* Warshay

Goldman, S. *See* Wells

Gordon, N. *See* Kutner

Greenblatt, M., Levinson, D., and Williams, R.: 123

Greenblum and Pearlin: 88-89

Greenstein, F.: 64

Gregory, W.: 70

Grigg, A. *See* Foster

Group: membership, 102-106; behavior, 106-16

Grusky, O.: success of prison indoctrination, 104; formal leaders and acceptance by authoritarians, 119

Gurin, G.: Veroff, J., and Feld, S., 38. *See also* A. Campbell

Haefner, D. *See* Haythorn

Hardyck, J. *See* Stein

Harned, L.: 59

Hart, I.: 73

Harvey, O.: used Webster, Sanford, Freedman scale, 32; summarized studies on topics in authoritarianism, 45-46; authoritarianism in relation to ego-involved objects and beliefs, 114; and Beverly, G., 101; and Caldwell, D., 44. *See also* B. White

Havel, J. *See* Christie

Hawkins, C. *See* Bass

Hax, H. *See* H. Leavitt

Haythorn, W., Couch, A., Haefner, D., Langham, P., and Carter, L.: behavior differences of authoritarians and non-authoritarians in small groups, 107; security and conflict in groups of varying authoritarianism, 115; characteristics of leaders from groups with high or low F scale scores, 116-17

Henry, W. *See* Cumming

Heron, A. *See* Carstairs

INDEX

Heslin, R.: 115

Hites, R., and Kellog, E.: used Webster, Sanford, Freedman scale, 32; found authoritarians favored segregation, 90

Hoffer, E.: 71

Hoffman, M.: 109

Hofstadter, R.: 62-64

Hollander, E. *See* Titus

Horowitz, M. *See* Centers

Hoult, T. *See* Stewart

Hover, G. *See* Lichtenstein

Huffman, P. *See* Levinson

Hyman, H.: 48; —and Sheatsley, P.: criticized *The Authoritarian Personality*, 7, 31-32, 35; relationship of E and F scales, 85

Ideology: role in voters' choice, 58; attitude not part of group ideology, 61-62; importance of, 62

Intolerance: associated more with political right than left, 57-58; and F scale, 93-94. *See also* "Ethnic Beliefs and Intolerance," 84-92

Jackman, A. *See* Fillenbaum

Jackson, D.—and Messick, S.: 17; — Messick, S., and Solly, C.: item reversal in F scale, 17; found response bias in both F scale scores and rigidity measures, 43

Jacobs, R. *See* Leventhal

Jahoda, M. *See* Christie

Janowitz, M.: and Marvick, D., 59. *See also* Bettelheim

Jensen, A.: 53

Jessor, R. *See* Roberts

Johnson, A. *See* Photiadis

Johnson, C. *See* R. Johnson

Johnson, H. *See* Steiner

Johnson, R.: Johnson, C., and Martin, L., 77. *See also* McCarthy

Jones, E.: 83-84

Jones, M.: 104-105

Kahn, R., Wolfe, D., Quinn, R., Snoek, J., and Rosenthal, R.: 120-21

Kaiman, I. *See* Vidulich

Kates, S., and Diab, L.: 73

Katz, D.—McClintock, C., and Sarnoff, I.: defensiveness and change to favorable attitudes, 97-98, 99; paranoid scales related to F scale measures of ego-defensiveness, 99; differences in response to attempts at influencing, 129; —and Stotland, E.: 97. *See also* Sarnoff; Stotland

Katz, I., and Benjamin, L.: 111-13

Kaufman, W.: 89

Kellog, E. *See* Hites

Kelman, H., and Barclay, J.: authoritarianism as function of capacity and experience, 9-10; found Negroes high on authoritarian measures, 37

Keniston, K. *See* Couch

Kenny, D., and Ginsberg, R.: 43

Kerlinger, F., and Rokeach, M.: 12

Knopfelmacher, F., and Armstrong, D.: 71-72

Kogan, N.: 52

Krug, R.: 31

Kudirka, N. *See* Leventhal

Kutner, B., and Gordon, N.: 86

Landes, J. *See* Cowen

Lane, R.: 59

Langham, P. *See* Haythorn

Lasky, J.: 109

Leadership: 116-26

Leavitt, G. *See* Gage

Leavitt, H., Hax, H., and Roche, J.: item reversal in F scale, 17; consistency in item reversal, 20-21; positive items enhancing F scale, 23

Leventhal, H., Jacobs, R., and Kudirka, N.: two studies of ideology in voters' choice, 58; ideology important for certain groups, 62

Levinson, D.: F scale, 33; developed scale for measuring nationalism, 65; and Gallagher, E., 124; —and Huffman, P: developed Traditional Family Ideology Scale, 33; TFI

INDEX

Levinson (*continued*):
scale scores positively related to F scale, 72-73. *See also* Adorno; Gilbert; Greenblatt; Pine

Levitt, E.: and Zuckerman, M., 43. *See also* Lyle

Liberalism. *See* Conservatism-liberalism

Libo, L.: 61-62

Lichtenstein, E., Quinn, R., and Hover, G.: 22

Lipset, S.: found lower classes less democratic, 39; emphasized difference in conservatism between economic and other areas, 58; authoritarianism in lower classes, 61, 62; predisposing factors same for authoritarian and religious beliefs, 70; working class authoritarianism, 78; social conditions contributing to authoritarianism, 127

Lipsitz, L.: found lower classes less democratic, 39; found education changed relationship between social class and authoritarianism, 40

Lundy, R. *See* Berkowitz

Lyle, W., and Levitt, E.: 74-75

McCandless, B. *See* D. Campbell

McCarthy, J., and Johnson, R.: 62

McClintock, C.: 98, 99. *See also* D. Katz

McClosky, H.: found party allegiance unrelated to authoritarianism, 58; found little relationship between conservatism and party affiliation, 59-60

McCormack, T. *See* D. Campbell

McDill, E.: compared social class and F scale scores, 37; associated anomia with lower economic status, 38; found F scale negatively related to education, 40; anomia and F scale scores related to prejudice, 90; alienation and authoritarianism related to ethnocentrism, 128

McGehee, C. *See* Bass

McGinnies, E. *See* Weiner

MacKinnon, W., and Centers, R: compared social class and F scale scores, 37-38; found F scale negatively related to education, 40; authoritarians and attitudes toward Russia, 66-67; punitive attitudes toward international relationships, 128-29

Mann, F. *See* Vroom

Martin, J.—and Westie, F.: linked ethnic intolerance with low status, 38; intolerance related to F scale scores, 88. *See also* Stanley

Martin, L. *See* R. Johnson

Marvick, D. *See* Janowitz

Maslow, A.: 5

Medalia, N: 118-19

Meidinger, T. *See* Crockett

Melikian, L. *See* E. Prothro

Mental illness: Custodial Mental Illness Scale, 121

Messick, S.: and Frederiksen, N., 17. *See also* Jackson

Miller, S., and Riessman, F.: 39

Miller, W. *See* A. Campbell

Millon, T.: 43-44

Mischel, W., and Schopler, J.: 44

Mowry, H.: 118

Mussen, P. *See* Scodel

Nadler, E: 108-109

Nationalism: defined, 65; Levinson's scale for, 65; mediates way aggression fastens on foreign affairs, 68

Niems, R., and Scodel, A.: 83

Niyekawa, A.: 36

Novak, E. *See* Fruchter

Occupation: 37-38

Open and Closed Mind, The: 12

Opinionation: 10-11. *See also* Dogmatism

Organization: 116-26

Paranoid style: 62-64

Parent Attitude Survey: 73

Participation in groups: 59

Patchen, M. *See* Stotland

INDEX

Rokeach (*continued*):
structural aspects of cognitive functioning, 94; dogmatic individual and differentiation of source and message, 111; alternative explanations to authoritarianism, 129; and Fruchter, B., 48. *See also* Fruchter; Kerlinger; Restle; Roberts

Role taking: cause of authoritarianism, 9, 129; and reaction of rigid person, 121

Rorer, L.: questioned significance of response bias, 15-16; complexity of response bias, 21; questioned adequacy of F scale item reversal, 25; challenged single disposition concept of response bias, 25

Rose, A.: 36

Rosen, E. *See* H. Smith

Rosenberg, M.: developed "faith in people" scale, 67; authoritarians misanthropic and negative, 84

Rosenthal, R. *See* Kahn

Samelson, F.: 21

Sampling: 31, 32

Sanford, N.: on *The Authoritarian Personality*, 4, 7; F scale, 5; defined subparts of authoritarianism, 5-6. *See also* Adorno; Freedman; Webster

Sarnoff, I: and Katz, D., 97. *See also* D. Katz

Schaet, D. *See* Cowen

Schopler, J. *See* Mischel

Schulberg, H.: content on response bias, 16; attributed F scale scores, 82-83; authoritarians and self-ratings, 83

Schutz, W.: 114-15

Schwab, J. *See* P. Adams

Scodel, A.: and Freedman, M., 82; and Mussen, P., 82. *See also* Niems

Scott, F. *See* Toobert

Seidenberg, B. *See* Christie

Sex: concern with, 6

Sheatsley, P. *See* Hyman

Shelley, H.: 14

Sherman, S.: 99

Shils, E.: F scale and political right, 10; concluded F scale studies dealt with right wing only, 57; fundamentalists and authoritarianism, 70-71

Siegel, A., and Siegel, S.: 102-103

Siegel, S.: 51. *See also* A. Siegel

Siegman, A.: 86

Simon, W.: 10

Simpson, G., and Yinger, J.: 87

Smith, C., and Prothro, J.: 37

Smith, H., and Rosen, E.: 65-66

Smith, M.: response bias, 13; distinguished response bias from authoritarianism, 25; designed F scale to avoid response bias, 32-33, 34; Bruner, J., and White, R., 97. *See also* Stein

Snoek, J. *See* Kahn

Social behavior: 95-126

Social characteristics: 35-42

Social mobility: 88-89

Social perception: 81-84

Solley, C. *See* Jackson

Solomon, A.: 105

Srole, L.: compared social class and F scale scores, 37; defined anomia, 38; found F scale negatively related to education, 40; anomia related to prejudice and F scale scores, 89-90

Stagner, R.: 5

Stanley, G., and Martin, J.: 22

Status: relation to authoritarianism, 37-39; concern with and antisemitism, 89; high and low status living groups and changes in F scale scores, 102-103; as determinant of response selection, 113-14

Steckler, G.: 37

Stein, D., Hardyck, J., and Smith, M.: 92

Steiner, I.—and Johnson, H.: F scale related to categorizing people "good" or "bad," 84; study using variations in conformity situation, 110; —and Vannoy, J.: 109

167

INDEX

Stember, C.: found educated groups more prejudiced in certain areas, 39; found education related differently to prejudice, 40-41, 89
Stereotypy: 6
Stewart, D., and Hoult, T.: role mastery, 9; role-taking ability, 129
Stokes, D. See A. Campbell
Stone, G. See Gage
Stotland, E.: Katz, D., and Patchen, M.: 98-99. See also D. Katz
Stouffer, S.: 38
Submission: authoritarian, defined, 6; explanation of response bias, 23-24
Sullivan, P., and Adelson, J.: authoritarians misanthropic and negative, 84; E scale positively related to misanthropy
Superstition: 6

Takezawa, S. See Triandis
Taylor, M. See Gladstone
Telford, C. See Plant
Thibaut, J., and Riecken, H.: 113
Thomas, J. See Plant
Titus, H., and Hollander, E.: reviewed F scale, 8-9; measures of authoritarianism relate most to other paper-and-pencil measures, 130
Toobert, S., Scott, F., and Lewis, J.: 123-24
Traditional Family Ideology Scale: use, 33; agreement with F scale, 72-73
Triandis, H.: Davis, E., and Takezawa, S., 36-37; and Triandis, L., 90-91, 92

Vannoy, J. See Steiner
Vaughan, G., and White, K.: used Berkowitz and Wolkon forced-choice F scale, 32; conformity associated with high authoritarianism measures, 109
Veroff, J. See Gurin

Vidulich, R.: and Kaiman, I., 111. See also H. Adams
Vroom, V.: 129; and Mann, F., 119-20

Wagman, M.: attitude change geared to predominant motivation, 97; cognitive restructuring and attitude change, 99-101
Warshay, L., Goldman, M., and Biddle, E.: 70
Webster, H.: Sanford, N., and Freedman, M., 32. See also Freedman
Weiner, N., and McGinnies, E.: 109, 110
Weinert, G. See Wells
Wells, W.—Chiaravallo, G., and Goldman, S.: fraternities ranked on intolerance, 103; authoritarian climate correlated with average F scale scores for fraternity members, 121; —Weinert, G., and Rubel, M.: 109
Westie, F. See J. Martin
White, B., and Harvey, O.: 45
White, J., Alter, R., and Rardin, M.: 45
White, K. See Vaughan
White, R. See M. Smith
Williams, C.: 62. See also E. Williams
Williams, E., and Williams, C.: 76
Williams, R. See Greenblatt
Wolfe, D. See Kahn
Wolkon, G. See N. Berkowitz

Xenophobia: 85-86
Yeasayers and naysayers: 20-21
Yinger, J. See Simpson
Young, P. See Bass

Zagona, S., and Zurcher, L.: 107-108
Zuckerman, M., and Eisen, B.: 24. See also Leavitt
Zurcher, L. See Zagona